Houghton Mifflin

CALIFORN

Math
Expressions

Volume 1

**Developed by
The Children's Math Worlds
Research Project**

PROJECT DIRECTOR AND AUTHOR

Dr. Karen C. Fuson

This material is based upon work supported by the
National Science Foundation
under Grant Numbers
ESI-9816320, REC-9806020, and RED-935373.

Any opinions, findings, and conclusions or recommendations expressed in this
material are those of the author and do not necessarily reflect the views of the
National Science Foundation.

 HOUGHTON MIFFLIN   BOSTON

Teacher Reviewers

Kindergarten
Patricia Stroh Sugiyama
Wilmette, Illinois

Barbara Wahle
Evanston, Illinois

Grade 1
Sandra Budson
Newton, Massachusetts

Janet Pecci
Chicago, Illinois

Megan Rees
Chicago, Illinois

Grade 2
Molly Dunn
Danvers, Massachusetts

Agnes Lesnick
Hillside, Illinois

Rita Soto
Chicago, Illinois

Grade 3
Jane Curran
Honesdale, Pennsylvania

Sandra Tucker
Chicago, Illinois

Grade 4
Sara Stoneberg Llibre
Chicago, Illinois

Sheri Roedel
Chicago, Illinois

Grade 5
Todd Atler
Chicago, Illinois

Leah Barry
Norfolk, Massachusetts

Special Thanks

Special thanks to the many teachers, students, parents, principals, writers, researchers, and work-study students who participated in the Children's Math Worlds Research Project over the years.

Credits

Cover art: (koala) © Royalty-Free/Corbis. (zebra) © Masahiro Iijima/Ardea London Ltd. (eucalyptus) © Victoria Pearson/Stone/Getty Images. (blocks) © HMCo./Richard Hutchings.

Illustrative art: Ginna Magee and Burgandy Beam/Wilkinson Studio; Tim Johnson
Technical art: Anthology, Inc.

Printed in the U.S.A.

ISBN-13: 978-0-618-89603-5
ISBN-10: 0-618-89603-1

3 4 5 6 7 8 9   KDL   11 10 09

VOLUME 1 CONTENTS

* This lesson consists only of activities from the Teacher's Guide.

Unit 3 Story Problem Strategies

Unit 4 Basic Ten-Structured Concepts

* This lesson consists only of activities from the Teacher's Guide.

Unit 5 Ten-Structured Applications

* This lesson consists only of activities from the Teacher's Guide.

Find the plates with 2 apples. Color the plates yellow.

Find the plate with 1 apple. Color the plate green.

Find the plates with 0 apples. Color the plates red.

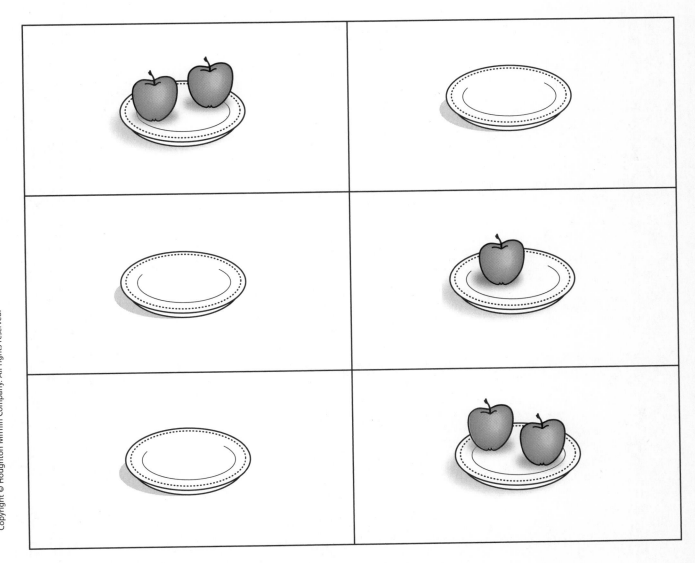

 On the Back Draw 2 apples.

Relate Math to Children's Lives

Dear Family:

Your child is learning math in an innovative program that interweaves abstract mathematical concepts with the everyday experiences of children. This helps children understand math better.

In this program, your child will learn math and have fun by

- working with objects and making drawings of math situations.
- working with other students and sharing problem-solving strategies with them.
- writing and solving problems and connecting math to daily life.
- helping classmates learn.

Your child will have homework almost every day. He or she needs a **Homework Helper.** The helper may be anyone—you, an older brother or sister (or other family member), a neighbor, or a friend. Make a specific time for homework and provide your child with a quiet place to work (for example, no TV). Encourage your child to talk about what is happening in math class. If your child is having problems with math, please talk to the teacher to see how you might help.

Thank you. You are vital to your child's learning.

Sincerely,
Your child's teacher

- -

Please fill out the following information and return this form to the teacher.

My child _____ will have _____
(child's name)   (Homework Helper's name)

as his or her Homework Helper. This person is my

child's _____.
(relationship to child)

Carta a la familia

Estimada familia:

Su niño está aprendiendo matemáticas con un programa innovador que relaciona conceptos matemáticos abstractos con la experiencia diaria de los niños. Esto ayuda a los niños a entender mejor las matemáticas.

Con este programa, su niño aprenderá matemáticas y se divertirá mientras

• trabaja con objetos y hace dibujos de problemas matemáticos.

• trabaja con otros estudiantes y comparte estrategias para resolver problemas.

• escribe y resuelve problemas y relaciona las matemáticas con la vida diaria.

• ayuda a sus compañeros a aprender.

Su niño tendrá tarea casi todos los días y necesita a una persona que lo ayude con la tarea. Esa persona puede ser usted, un hermano mayor (u otro familiar), un vecino o un amigo. Establezca una hora para la tarea y ofrezca a su niño un lugar tranquilo donde trabajar (por ejemplo un lugar sin TV). Anime a su niño a comentar lo que está aprendiendo en la clase de matemáticas. Si su niño tiene problemas con las matemáticas, por favor hable con el maestro para ver cómo puede ayudarlo.

Muchas gracias. Usted es imprescindible en el aprendizaje de su niño.

Atentamente,
El maestro de su niño

- -

Por favor escriba la siguiente información y devuelva este formulario al maestro.

La persona que ayudará a mi niño _____ es
(nombre del niño)

_____. Esta persona es _____
(nombre de la persona)   (relación con el niño)

de mi niño.

Relate Math to Children's Lives

1–2

Class Activity

Name _____

Vocabulary
patterns

Write the numbers.

1. | 0 | 0 | 0 | 0 | 0 | 0 | | | | | | | | | | | |
   | 0 | | | | | | | | | | | | | | | | |

2. | I | I | I | I | I | I | | | | | | | | | | | |
   | I | | | | | | | | | | | | | | | | |

3. | 2 | 2 | 2 | 2 | 2 | 2 | | | | | | | | | | | |
   | 2 | | | | | | | | | | | | | | | | |

Repeat the **patterns**.

4. I 2 I 2

5. | ● | ○ | ● | ○ | ● | ○ | | | | | | | | | | | |

Write how many.

6. How many hats?	**7.** How many hats?	**8.** How many hats?
 ☐	☐	 ☐

➡ **On the Back** Draw 2 stick people with 0 hats.

UNIT I LESSON 2   CA Standards: KEY NS 1.1; KEY SDAP 2.1   Numbers and Patterns: 0, I, 2 **5**

Numbers and Patterns: 0, I, 2

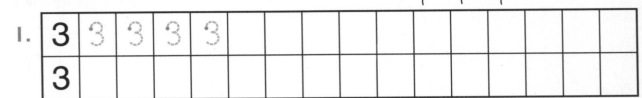

Class Activity

Name _____

Vocabulary
triangles

Write number 3.

1.

3	3	3	3	3										
3														

Repeat the patterns.

2.

| 1 | 2 | 3 | | | | | | | | | | | | |

3.

4.

| ll | = | ll | = | ll | = | | | | | | | | | |

Color the **triangles**. Count how many.

5.

How many? ☐

6.

How many?

7.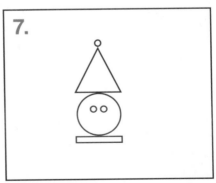

How many?

8.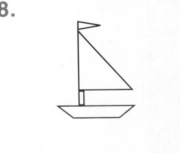

How many?

⬤ **On the Back** Draw some triangles.

Relate Numbers and Shapes: Number 3

Class Activity

Name _____

Vocabulary
rectangle

Write number 4.

1. | 4 | 4 | 4 | 4 | 4 | | | | | | | | | | |
   |---|---|---|---|---|---|---|---|---|---|---|---|---|---|---|
   | 4 | | | | | | | | | | | | | | |

Repeat the patterns.

2. | 1 | 2 | 3 | 4 | 1 | 2 | 3 | 4 | | | | | | | |

3. | 2 | 3 | 2 | 3 | 2 | 3 | 2 | 3 | | | | | | | |

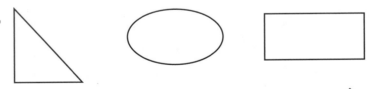

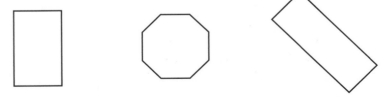

Color the **rectangles**. Count how many.

6.

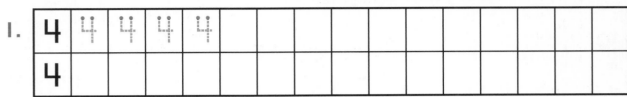

How many? ☐

Extra Practice

Color 4 hearts.

1.

Color 4 suns.

2.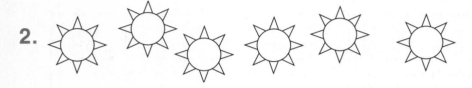

Color 4 moons.

3.

Color the rectangles.

4.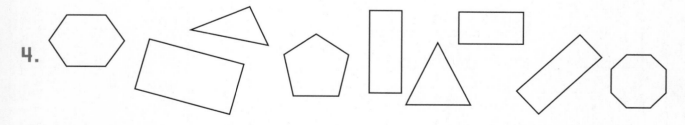

Make a pattern with 2 colors.

5.

Relate Numbers and Shapes: Number 4

Name _____

Class Activity

Place 4 counters in a row here.

1.

Draw the break-apart line. Color the circles to show the 4-partners.
Write the numbers.

2. ○○○○ | + | $4 = 1 + 3$

○○○○ | + | $4 = 2 + 2$

○○○○ | + | $4 = 3 + 1$

Show the 4-partners as a train.

3.

🔵 **On the Back** Make up a repeated pattern.

Partners and Totals: Number 4

Dear Family:

Your child is starting to discover the smaller numbers that are "hiding" inside a larger number. He or she will be participating in activities that help your child master addition, subtraction, and equation building.

To make the concepts clear, this program uses some special vocabulary and materials that we would like to share. Below are two important words that your child is learning:

• **Partners:** Partners are two numbers that can be put together to make a larger number. For example, 2 and 5 are partners that go together to make the number 7.

• **Break Apart:** Children can "break apart" a larger number to form two smaller numbers. Your child is using objects and drawings to explore ways of "breaking apart" numbers of ten or less.

Children can discover the break-aparts of a number by coloring circles in two colors. They first draw the "break-apart line" and then color the circles to show the different partners, as shown below. Sometimes they also write the partners on a special break-apart train, which is also shown below.

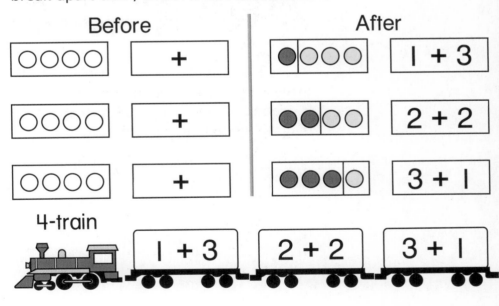

Later children will discover that partners can change places without changing the total. This concept is called "switch the partner." Once children understand switching partners, they can find the break-aparts of a number more quickly. They simply switch each pair of partners as they discover them.

Shown below are the break-aparts and switched partners of number 7. Sometimes children also write this information on a double-decker train.

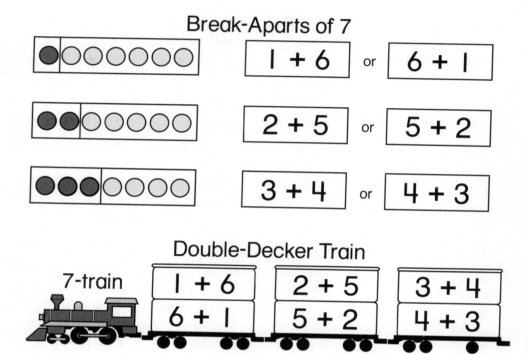

Break-Aparts of 7

| 1 + 6 | or | 6 + 1 |

| 2 + 5 | or | 5 + 2 |

| 3 + 4 | or | 4 + 3 |

Double-Decker Train

7-train

| 1 + 6 | 2 + 5 | 3 + 4 |
| 6 + 1 | 5 + 2 | 4 + 3 |

You will see the break-apart circles and the break-apart train often on your child's math homework. Be ready to offer help if it is needed. Children are doing these activities in class, but they may still need help at home.

If you have any questions or problems, please talk to your child's teacher.

Sincerely,
Your child's teacher

Partners and Totals: Number 4

Estimada familia:

Su niño está empezando a descubrir los números más pequeños que están "escondidos" dentro de un número más grande. Va a participar en actividades que le ayudarán a dominar la suma, la resta y la formación de ecuaciones.

Para clarificar los conceptos, este programa usa un vocabulario especial y algunos materiales que nos gustaría mostrarle. A continuación hay dos palabras importantes que su niño está aprendiendo:

- **Partes**: Partes son dos números que se pueden unir para formar un número más grande. Por ejemplo, 2 y 5 son partes que se unen para formar el número 7.

- **Separar**: Los niños pueden "separar" un número más grande para formar dos números más pequeños. Su niño está usando objetos y dibujos para explorar maneras de "separar" números iguales o menores que diez.

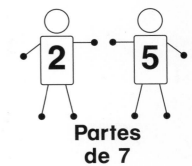

Partes de 7

Los niños pueden encontrar las partes de un número coloreando círculos con dos colores. Primeo dibujan la "línea de separación" y luego colorean los círculos para indicar las partes, como se muestra a continuación. A veces los niños anotan las partes en un tren de partes especial, que también se muestra a continuación.

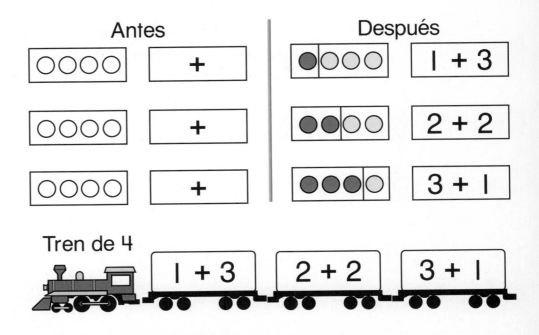

Luego los niños van a aprender que las partes pueden intercambiar su posición sin que varíe el total. Este concepto se llama "cambiar el orden de las partes". Una vez que los niños entienden el cambio del orden de las partes, pueden encontrar las partes de un número con más rapidez. Sencillamente cambian cada par de partes a medida que las encuentran.

A continuación están las partes y las partes en otro orden del número 7. A veces los niños escriben esta información en un tren de dos pisos.

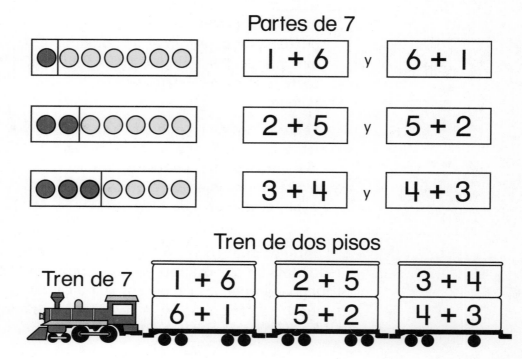

Partes de 7

1 + 6	y	6 + 1
2 + 5	y	5 + 2
3 + 4	y	4 + 3

Tren de dos pisos

Tren de 7

| 1 + 6 | 2 + 5 | 3 + 4 |
| 6 + 1 | 5 + 2 | 4 + 3 |

Usted verá con frecuencia los círculos y el tren de partes en la tarea de matemáticas de su niño. Sería aconsejable que le ofreciera ayuda si fuera necesario. Los niños están haciendo estas actividades en clase, pero es posible que necesiten más ayuda en casa.

Si tiene preguntas o dudas, por favor hable con el maestro de su niño.

Atentamente,
El maestro de su niño

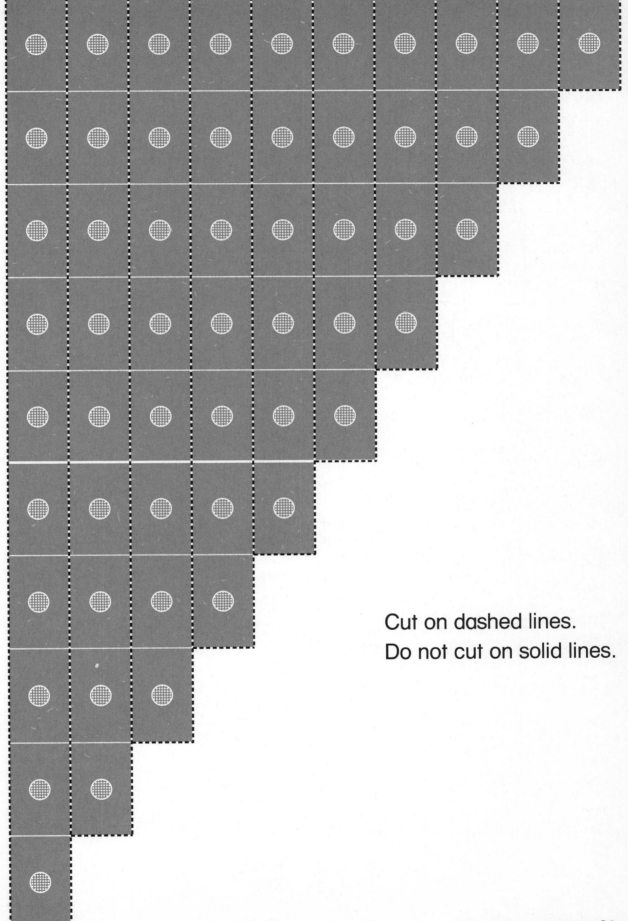

Cut on dashed lines.
Do not cut on solid lines.

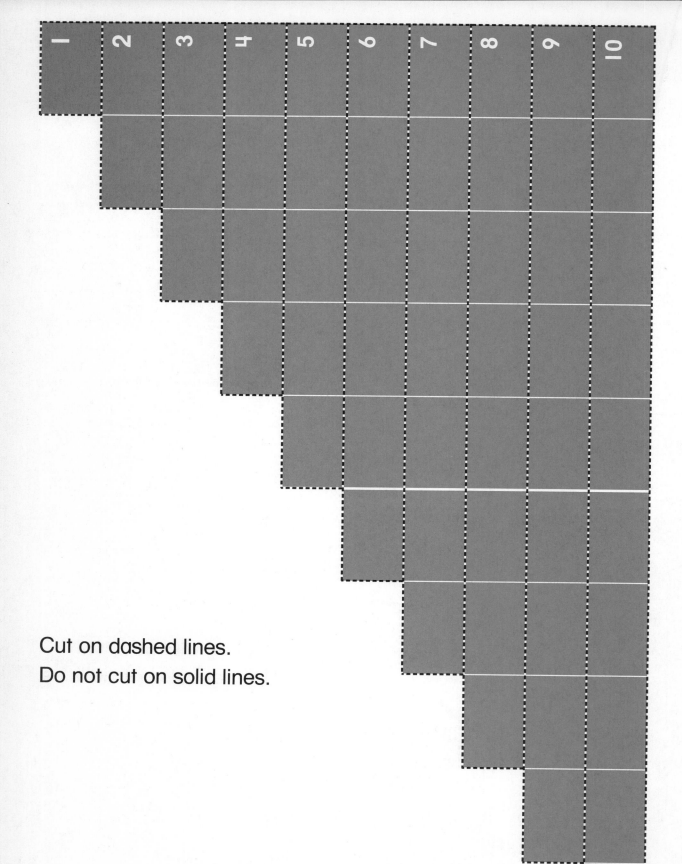

Cut on dashed lines.
Do not cut on solid lines.

Name _____

1. Use the Stair Steps to show the partners of 7.

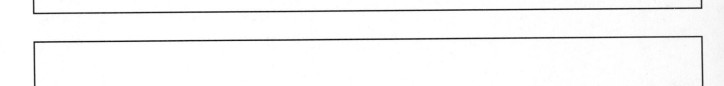

Stair Step 7

Show the 7-partners and the switched partners.

2. ○○○○○○○ [+] and [+]

3. ○○○○○○○ [+] and [+]

4. ○○○○○○○ [+] and [+]

5. Show the 7-partners as a double train.

7-train   [+ / +]   [+ / +]   [+ / +]

🔵 **On the Back** Draw a picture to show one set of partners of 7.

Add in Any Order

Class Activity

Name

Write the number 8.

1. | 8 | 8 | 8 | 8 | 8 | | | | | | | | | | | |
   |---|---|---|---|---|---|---|---|---|---|---|---|---|---|---|---|
   | 8 | | | | | | | | | | | | | | | |

Repeat the patterns.

2. | 7 | 8 | 7 | 8 | | | | | | | | | | | |
   |---|---|---|---|---|---|---|---|---|---|---|---|---|---|---|

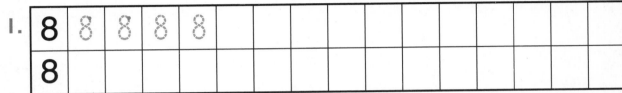

Show the 8-partners and **switch the partners**.

4. ○○○○○○○○ | + | and | + |

5. ○○○○○○○○ | + | and | + |

6. ○○○○○○○○ | + | and | + |

7. ○○○○○○○○ | + | and | + |

⬤ **On the Back** What are the **equal partners** for 8? Draw and write your answer.

Break-Aparts of Number 8

Class Activity

Name _____

Vocabulary
pattern
switch the partners

Write the number 9.

1. | 9 | 9 | 9 | 9 | 9 | | | | | | | | | |
   |---|---|---|---|---|---|---|---|---|---|---|---|---|---|
   | 9 | | | | | | | | | | | | | |

Repeat the **pattern**.

2. | 8 | 9 | 8 | 9 | | | | | | | | | | | |
   |---|---|---|---|---|---|---|---|---|---|---|---|---|---|---|

Show the 9-partners and **switch the partners**.

3. ○○○○○○○○○   + ___ and + ___

4. ○○○○○○○○○   + ___ and + ___

5. ○○○○○○○○○   + ___ and + ___

6. ○○○○○○○○○   + ___ and + ___

7. 9-train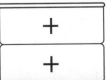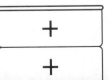

Going Further

Name _____

Color the cans to show **partners** of 9.

1.

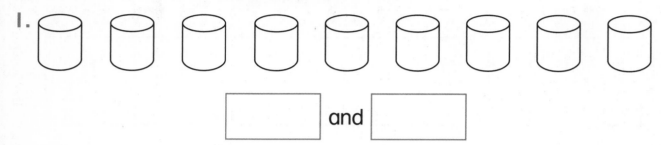

[ ] and [ ]

Color the faces to show different partners of 9.

2.

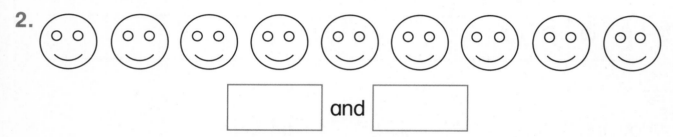

[ ] and [ ]

Use 3 numbers. Make a **pattern** that repeats.

3.

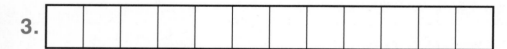

Use 2 shapes. Make a pattern that repeats.

4.

Use 2 colors. Make a color pattern that repeats.

5.

CA Standards: NS 1.3; KEY SDAP 2.1   Break-Aparts of Number 9

6

7

8

9

10

1

2

3

4

5

Number Cards 1–10

Dear Family:

Your child is learning to see numbers as a group of 5 and extra ones. Making mental pictures by grouping units in this way will later help your child add and subtract quickly. Children benefit greatly from learning to "see" numbers without counting every unit.

Children start exploring these 5-groups by looking at dots arranged in a row of 5 plus some extra ones. Below are samples that show the numbers from 6 through 10:

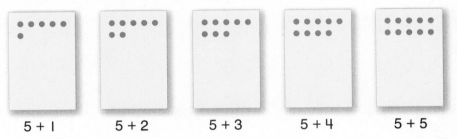

| 5 + 1 | 5 + 2 | 5 + 3 | 5 + 4 | 5 + 5 |

The teacher gives the children a number and asks them to say it as a 5 plus extra ones. Children say the numbers in order at first. Later they can "see" the quantities even when the numbers are shown randomly.

Teacher: What is 6?

Class: 5 + 1

Teacher: What is 7?

Class: 5 + 2

On some homework pages, you will find instructions that say, "See the 5." Your child is being encouraged to make a mental picture of a number that contains a 5-group. Later the children will be asked to see groups of 10 by combining two 5-groups. This will help them learn place value.

It takes repeated exposure to such groups for children to see the numbers quickly. Many of the visual aids in your child's classroom include 5-groups. Children tend to absorb these visual patterns without realizing it.

If you have any questions or problems, please contact me.

Sincerely,
Your child's teacher

Estimada familia:

Su niño está aprendiendo a ver los números como un grupo de 5 más otras unidades. El hecho de agrupar mentalmente unidades de esa manera ayudará a su niño a sumar y restar rápidamente en el futuro. Los niños se benefician muchísimo de aprender a "ver" los números sin contar cada unidad.

Los niños comienzan a practicar con estos grupos de 5 observando puntos distribuidos en una fila de 5 más otras unidades. Estos ejemplos muestran los números del 6 al 10:

El maestro les da un número a los niños y les pide que lo digan como 5 más otras unidades. Al principio, los niños dicen los números en orden. Más adelante

Maestro: ¿Qué es el 6?

Clase: 5 + 1

Maestro: ¿Qué es el 7?

Clase: 5 + 2

pueden "ver" las cantidades incluso cuando los números se muestran sin un orden específico.

En algunas páginas de la tarea encontrará instrucciones que dicen "Ve el número 5". A su niño se le está animando a que visualice un número que contenga un grupo de 5. Más adelante se les pedirá que vean grupos de 10, combinando dos grupos de 5. Esto les ayudará a aprender el valor posicional.

Es necesario que los niños practiquen muchas veces los grupos de este tipo para que puedan llegar a ver los números rápidamente. Muchas de las ayudas visuales que hay en el salón de clase incluyen grupos de 5. Los niños tienden a absorber estos patrones visuales sin darse cuenta.

Si tiene alguna pregunta o comentario, por favor comuníquese conmigo.

Atentamente,
El maestro de su niño

Visualize Numbers as a 5-Group and Ones

Name _____

Class Activity

Odd or **even** ? Ring one.

1.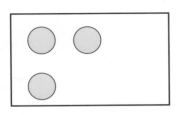

odd   even

2.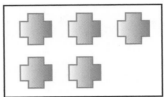

odd   even

3.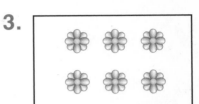

odd   even

4.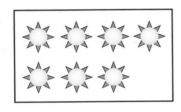

odd   even

5.

odd   even

6.

odd   even

Write the **equal partners** . Then write the **total** .

Total

7.   ☐ + ☐   ☐

8.    ☐ + ☐   ☐

9.    ☐ + ☐   ☐

10. ☐☐☐☐☐☐☐☐   ☐ + ☐   ☐

➡ **On the Back** Draw an even number of shapes. Then draw an odd number of shapes.

Exploration: Doubles and Even and Odd Numbers

Name _____

Repeat the patterns.

1.

2. | + | + | − | + | + | − | | | | | | | | |
|---|---|---|---|---|---|---|---|---|---|---|---|---|---|

3. | 7 | 8 | 9 | 7 | 8 | 9 | | | | | | | | |
|---|---|---|---|---|---|---|---|---|---|---|---|---|---|

4. Write number 8. ☐

5. Write number 5. ☐

6. Write number 2. ☐

7. Write number 10. ☐

8. How many airplanes? Write the number in the box.

☐

9. How many bottles? Write the number in the box.

☐

Draw the break-apart line. Color the circles to show the 3-partners. Write the partners.

10. ○ ○ ○ | ___ + ___

11. ○ ○ ○ | ___ + ___

 **Name** _____

Show the 7-partners and the switched partners

12. ⟨○ ○ ○ ○ ○ ○ ○⟩ | + | and | + |

13. ⟨○ ○ ○ ○ ○ ○ ○⟩ | + | and | + |

14. ⟨○ ○ ○ ○ ○ ○ ○⟩ | + | and | + |

Draw the rest of the dots in the empty box.

15. 6   16. 9   17. 7

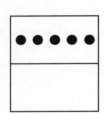   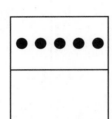   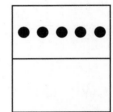

Odd or even? Ring one.

18.

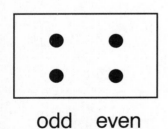

odd   even

19.

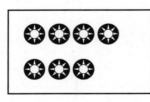

odd   even

20. Extended Response Draw 4 triangles.

Test

Class Activity

Name _____

Vocabulary
partners
total

Write the **partners** and the **total**.

1. [ ] + [ ]

Total [ ]

2. [ ] + [ ]

Total [ ]

3. [ ] + [ ]

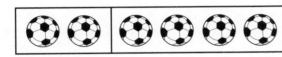

Total [ ]

4. [ ] + [ ]

Total [ ]

5. [ ] + [ ]

Total [ ]

6. [ ] + [ ]

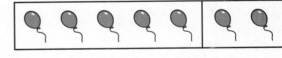

Total [ ]

➡ **7. On the Back** Draw a picture to show 6 + 2. Write the total.

Addition with Simple Pictures

Dear Family:

Your child has started a new unit on addition, subtraction, and equations. These concepts are introduced with stories that capture children's interest and help them to see adding and subtracting as real-life processes.

At the beginning of the unit, children show a story problem by drawing a picture of the objects. If they are adding 4 balloons and 2 balloons, for example, their pictures might look like the top one shown here.

Addition

Subtraction

In a short time, children will show objects quickly with circles rather than pictures. This is a major conceptual advance because it requires the use of symbols. Children are asked to show the parts (4 + 2) as well as give the answer (6). These circle drawings are similar to the break-apart drawings that are already familiar to them. From here, children are just a small step away from writing standard equations, such as 4 + 2 = 6.

$4 + 2$

$O O O O | O O$

6

Addition Problem

$6 - 4$

$\cancel{O}\cancel{O}\cancel{O}\cancel{O} | O O$

2

Subtraction Problem

To keep them focused on the actual problem, children are often asked to give a "complete answer" in class. This means that they should name the objects as well as give the number. Right now, complete answers are not required for homework. Even so, it would be helpful for you to ask your child to say the complete answer when working with you at home. Example: "You said the answer is 6. Is it 6 dinosaurs? No? Then 6 what? . . . Oh! 6 balloons!"

Sincerely,
Your child's teacher

Addition with Simple Pictures **43**

Estimada familia:

Su niño ha empezado una nueva unidad sobre la suma, la resta y las ecuaciones. Estos conceptos se presentan con cuentos que captan el interés de los niños y les ayudan a ver la suma y la resta como procesos de la vida diaria.

Al comienzo de la unidad, los niños muestran un problema en forma de cuento haciendo un dibujo de los objetos. Por ejemplo, si están sumando 4 globos y 2 globos, sus dibujos pueden parecerse al dibujo que se muestra aquí.

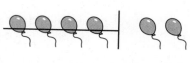

Al poco tiempo, los niños mostrarán objetos rápidamente con círculos en vez de dibujos. Esto es un gran paso conceptual, ya que requiere el uso de símbolos. A los niños se les pide que muestren las partes (4 + 2) y la respuesta (6). Estos dibujos con círculos se parecen a los dibujos de separaciones que ellos ya conocen. Una vez que hacen esto, están casi listos para escribir ecuaciones normales, tales como 4 + 2 = 6.

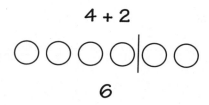

Problema de suma

Problema de resta

Para que sigan concentrándose en el problema mismo, a los niños se les pide una "respuesta completa" en la clase. Esto significa que deben nombrar los objetos y dar el número. Actualmente, no se requieren respuestas completas en la tarea. Sin embargo, sería de ayuda si le pidiera a su niño que le dé la respuesta completa cuando trabaja con Ud. en casa. Por ejemplo: "Dijiste que la respuesta es 6. ¿Son 6 dinosaurios? ¿No? Entonces, ¿6 de qué?. . . ¡Ajá! ¡6 globos!"

Atentamente,
El maestro de su niño

Addition with Simple Pictures

Class Activity

Vocabulary
partners
total

Write the **partners** and **total** for each circle drawing.

1.

Total ☐

2.

Total ☐

3.

Total ☐

4.

Total ☐

5.

Total ☐

6.

Total ☐

7. Show What circle drawing shows 5 + 5? Draw your answer below.

UNIT 2 LESSON 2   CA Standards: KEY NS 2.1   Addition with Circle Drawings **45**

Copyright © Houghton Mifflin Company. All rights reserved.

Going Further

Name _____

Vocabulary
circle drawings

Match the pictures to the **circle drawings**.

1.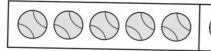

□ + □

●●●●● ○○

Total □

2.

□ + □

●● ○○○ ○○○

Total □

3.

□ + □

●●● ○○ ○○

Total □

4.

□ + □

 ●●●●● ● ○○○○

Total □

CA Standards: KEY NS 2.1

Addition with Circle Drawings

Name _____

Class Activity

Vocabulary
equation

Write the partners and the total. Then write the **equation**.

1.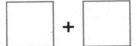

Total [ ]

_____
Equation

2.

Total [ ]

_____
Equation

3.

Total [ ]

_____
Equation

4.

Total [ ]

_____
Equation

➡ 5. **On the Back** Write two equations of your own.

Introduction to Addition Equations

Dear Family:

Earlier in the unit, your child solved addition problems by making math drawings and counting every object. Now your child is moving beyond drawings and is working with real equations. At this stage, children need a faster strategy that allows them to work directly with numbers. The method they are learning is called *counting on.* It is explained below.

In an addition problem such as 5 + 4, children say (or "think") the first number as if they had already counted it. Then they count on from there. The last number they say is the total. Children can keep track by raising a finger or making a dot for each number as they count on. The diagram below shows both the finger method and the dot method.

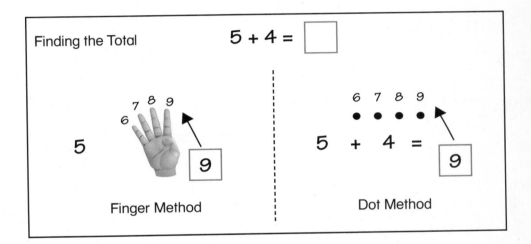

Counting on requires repeated practice. This is provided in class activities and homework assignments. Right now, your child is learning how to find unknown totals. In the next unit, he or she will learn to use a different Counting On strategy to subtract.

Counting on is a temporary method that children can use until they know all the math facts. Later, they will not need to count on at all, because they will automatically know the answer when the total is 10 or less.

Sincerely,
Your child's teacher

Estimada familia:

Un poco antes en la unidad su niño resolvió problemas de suma haciendo dibujos matemáticos y contando todos los objetos. Ahora su niño está progresando más allá de los dibujos y está trabajando con ecuaciones reales. En esta estapa, los niños necesitan una estrategia más rápida que les permita trabajar directamente con los números. El método que están aprendiendo se llama *contar hacia adelante.* Se explica a continuación.

En un problema de suma, como 5 + 4, los niños dicen (o "piensan") el primer número como si ya lo hubieran contado. Luego cuentan hacia adelante a partir de él. El último número que dicen es el total. Los niños pueden llevar la cuenta levantando un dedo o haciendo un punto por cada número mientras cuentan hacia adelante. El diagrama a continuación muestra tanto el método de los dedos como el de los puntos.

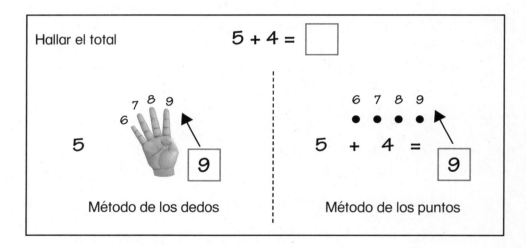

Contar hacia adelante requiere práctica repetida. Esto sucede en las actividades de clase y en las tareas. En esta unidad, su niño está aprendiendo a hallar un total desconocido. En la próxima unidad, aprenderá a usar otra estrategia de contar hacia adelante para restar.

Contar hacia adelante es un método que los niños pueden usar hasta que sepan todas las operaciones básicas. Más adelante no les hará falta contar hacia adelante porque automáticamente van a saber la respuesta cuando el total es 10 ó menos.

Atentamente,
El maestro de su niño

Explore Solution Methods

Class Activity

Name _____

Vocabulary
total
equation

Complete the exercises.

1. 4 + 3 = ☐   2. 6 + 4 = ☐   3. 4 + 4 = ☐

4. 5 + 4 = ☐   5. 5 + 3 = ☐   6. 8 + 2 = ☐

7. 2 + 3 = ☐   8. 7 + 3 = ☐   9. 3 + 3 = ☐

Find the **total** number of toys in each group.

10. 3 cars in the box

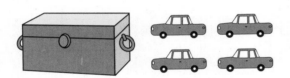

☐ Total

11. 7 boats in the box

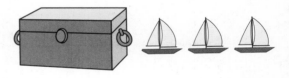

☐ Total

12. 6 dolls in the box

☐ Total

13. 5 balls in the box

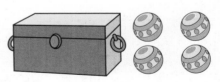

☐ Total

➡ 14. **On the Back** Write three equations
that show a total of 10.

Name

Addition Strategies: Counting On

Class Activity

Name _____

Vocabulary
cents
Nickel Strip

Write how many **cents** in each group.
Use your **Nickel Strip** to check your work.

1.
☐ ¢

2.
☐ ¢

3.
☐ ¢

4.
☐ ¢

5.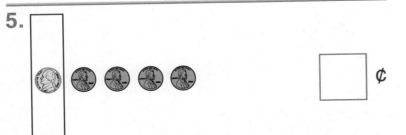
☐ ¢

Nickel Strip

<u>Cut</u> on dashed lines.
<u>Fold</u> on solid line
and tape at top and
bottom.

Nickels, Pennies, and Counting On

Class Activity

Name _____

Vocabulary
greater number
count on
nickel
cents

Underline the **greater number** .
Count on from that number.

1.

$3 + \underline{7} =$ ☐

2.

$4 + 5 =$ ☐

3.

$2 + 6 =$ ☐

4.

$5 + 3 =$ ☐

5.

$7 + 2 =$ ☐

6.

$3 + 6 =$ ☐

Count on from the **nickel** . Write how many **cents** .

7.   = ☐ ¢

8.   = ☐ ¢

9. **Tell Why** Show two ways to count on to find the total of $6 + 3$.
Which is faster?

☐

Name _____

Going Further

Vocabulary
pattern

Extend the **pattern**.

1.

2.

3.

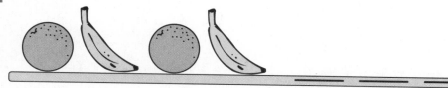

4.

5. Make Your Own Pattern Draw your pattern in the box.
Describe your pattern using letters.

CA Standards: **KEY SDAP 2.1**

Count On from the Greater Number

$3 + 3 = \boxed{}$ $3 + 4 = \boxed{}$ $3 + 5 = \boxed{}$

$3 + 6 = \boxed{}$ $3 + 7 = \boxed{}$ $4 + 3 = \boxed{}$

$4 + 4 = \boxed{}$ $4 + 5 = \boxed{}$ $4 + 6 = \boxed{}$

$5 + 3 = \boxed{}$ $5 + 4 = \boxed{}$ $5 + 5 = \boxed{}$

$6 + 3 = \boxed{}$ $6 + 4 = \boxed{}$ $7 + 3 = \boxed{}$

$3 + 5 = \boxed{8}$

•••	5

$3 + 4 = \boxed{7}$

•••	4

$3 + 3 = \boxed{6}$

3	•••

$4 + 3 = \boxed{7}$

4	•••

$3 + 7 = \boxed{10}$

•••	7

$3 + 6 = \boxed{9}$

•••	6

$4 + 6 = \boxed{10}$

••••	6

$4 + 5 = \boxed{9}$

••••	5

$4 + 4 = \boxed{8}$

4	••••

$5 + 5 = \boxed{10}$

5	•••••

$5 + 4 = \boxed{9}$

5	••••

$5 + 3 = \boxed{8}$

5	•••

$7 + 3 = \boxed{10}$

7	•••

$6 + 4 = \boxed{10}$

6	••••

$6 + 3 = \boxed{9}$

6	•••

Red Count-On Cards

Number Quilt 1: Unknown Totals

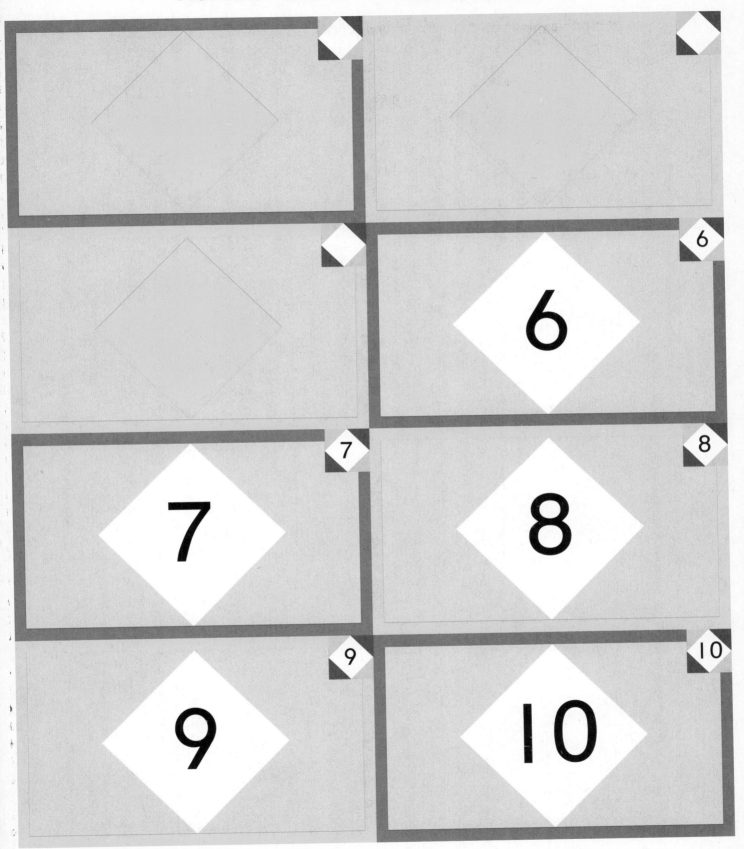

Use with the Red Count-On Cards.

Extra Practice

Name _____

Color the pictures. Draw more to **count on**.

Write how many in all.

1.

$4 + 1 = \boxed{}$

2.

$6 + 2 = \boxed{}$

3.

$3 + 3 = \boxed{}$

4.

$5 + 4 = \boxed{}$

5.

$7 + 3 = \boxed{}$

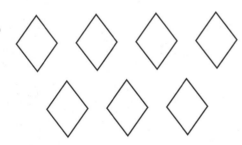 **6. On the Back** Use shapes to draw an addition picture for
$6 + 3 = \boxed{}$. Write how many in all.

CA Standards: KEY NS 2.1

Addition Game: Unknown Totals

Extra Practice

Vocabulary
coins
equation

Name

Count the **coins**. Match.

1.    4¢

2.    6¢

3. 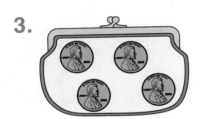   7¢

4.    9¢

5.    8¢

6. ➡ **On the Back** Draw a nickel and some pennies. Write an **equation** to show the total number of cents.

Class Activity

Name

1. There were 8 apples.

Then 5 were eaten.

$8 - 5 = \boxed{}$

---

2. There were 9 flowers.

Then 4 were picked.

$9 - 4 = \boxed{}$

---

3. There were 6 dolphins.

Then 3 swam away.

$6 - 3 = \boxed{}$

---

4. There were 10 balloons.

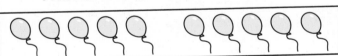

Then 6 popped.

$10 - 6 = \boxed{}$

5. On the Back You have 7 balls.
You lose 2 balls. How many balls are left?
Write your answer on the back.

Introduction to Subtraction

Class Activity

Vocabulary
subtract
solve

1. ⬭ ◯◯◯◯◯ ◯◯◯◯ ⬭

   Subtract 5   Equation _____

2. ⬭ ◯◯◯◯◯ ◯◯◯◯◯ ⬭

   Subtract 4   Equation _____

3. ⬭ ◯◯◯◯◯ ◯◯ ⬭

   Subtract 3   Equation _____

4. ⬭ ◯◯◯◯◯ ◯◯◯◯◯ ⬭

   Subtract 8   Equation _____

5. ⬭ ◯◯◯◯◯ ◯◯◯ ⬭

   Subtract 5   Equation _____

➡ 6. **On the Back** There are 6 marbles on the table.
   4 marbles roll off. How many marbles are there
   now? Use a circle drawing to **solve**.

Subtraction with Drawings and Equations

2-13 Extra Practice

Name ___

Use the picture to solve the **equation**.

1. $9 - 6 = \square$

2. $8 - 5 = \square$

3. $4 - 4 = \square$

4. $7 - 3 = \square$

5. $6 - 5 = \square$

6. $5 - 4 = \square$

7. $10 - 6 = \square$

8. $9 - 3 = \square$

9. $7 - 6 = \square$

10. $10 - 2 = \square$

11. **On the Back** Make a **circle drawing** for the equation $6 - 2 = \square$. Then find the answer.

Practice with Subtraction

Name _____

Going Further

1. Ring the puppy that Miguel would pick.

I like spots.
I like long fur.

⇨ **On the Back** Mia wants a green kite that is shaped like a square. Draw a kite that Mia will pick. Then draw a kite that she will not pick.

Generate Subtraction Problems

Class Activity

Name _____

Add the numbers.

1.	2.	3.	4.	5.
8	5	2	6	4
+ 2 • •	+ 3	+ 7	+ 4	+ 4

Use the pictures. Subtract the numbers.

6.

$8 - 3 = \boxed{}$

$$\begin{array}{r} 8 \\ - 3 \\ \hline \end{array}$$

7.

$10 - 4 = \boxed{}$

$$\begin{array}{r} 10 \\ - 4 \\ \hline \end{array}$$

8.

$9 - 5 = \boxed{}$

$$\begin{array}{r} 9 \\ - 5 \\ \hline \end{array}$$

9.

$7 - 4 = \boxed{}$

$$\begin{array}{r} 7 \\ - 4 \\ \hline \end{array}$$

10. On the Back Make up your own subtraction equation. Write it two ways on the back.

CA Standards: KEY NS 2.1 Addition and Subtraction Equations Written in Vertical Form **73**

Addition and Subtraction Equations Written in Vertical Form

Name _____

Unit Test 2

Write how many cents in each group.

1.   ☐ ¢

2.   ☐ ¢

Write the cost of the toys together.

3.

☐ + ☐ = ☐ ¢

4.

☐ + ☐ = ☐ ¢

Write the partners and the total for each picture.

5. ☐ + ☐

Total ☐

6. ☐ + ☐

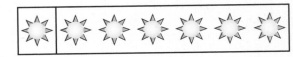

Total ☐

7. ☐ + ☐

Total ☐

8. ☐ + ☐

Total ☐

UNIT 2

Write the partners and total. Then write the equation.

9. ☐ **+** ☐

Total ☐

_____
Equation

10. ☐ **+** ☐

Total ☐

_____
Equation

Count on. Write the total.

11.  **=** ☐   Total

12.  **=** ☐   Total

Use the pictures. Subtract the numbers.

13.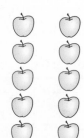

$$\begin{array}{r} 10 \\ -\ 5 \\ \hline \end{array}$$

14.

$$\begin{array}{r} 6 \\ -\ 2 \\ \hline \end{array}$$

Test

Name _____

Write how many are left. Use the picture to help you.

15.   There were 10 crayons.

       Then 2 were lost.

$10 - 2 = \boxed{}$

---

16.   There were 7 sailboats.

       Then 3 sailed away.

$7 - 3 = \boxed{}$

Subtract and write the equation.

17.   ⭕⭕⭕⭕⭕   ⭕⭕⭕⭕

       Subtract 4   _____

                        Equation

18.   ⭕⭕⭕⭕⭕   ⭕

       Subtract 3   _____

                        Equation

19.   ⭕⭕⭕⭕⭕   ⭕⭕⭕⭕

       Subtract 8   _____

                        Equation

Name _____

Add the numbers.

20. 5 + 4 = ☐   **21.** 2 + 6 = ☐   **22.** 3 + 3 = ☐

Subtract the numbers.

23. 5 − 3 = ☐   **24.** 8 − 7 = ☐

25. Extended Response Draw circles to show 5 + 4. Then write
an equation that shows the partner and the total.

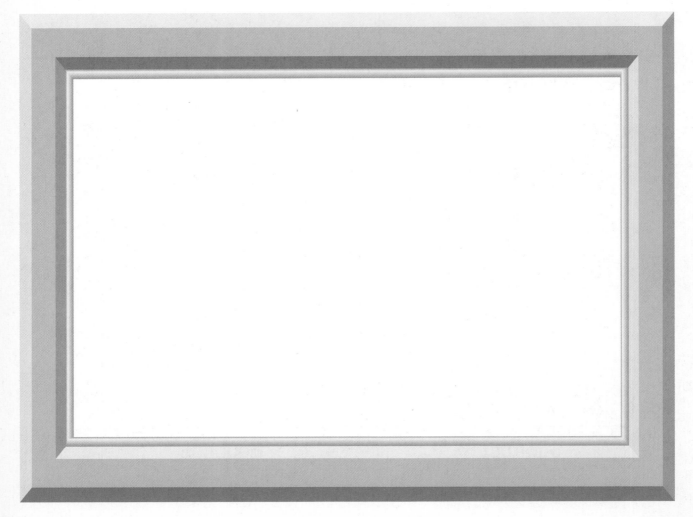

Class Activity

Name _____

Vocabulary
unknown partner
Math Mountains

Find the **unknown partner**.

1.

6
4 + ☐

2.
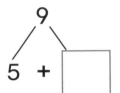
9
5 + ☐

3.
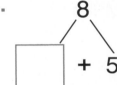
8
☐ + 5

4.
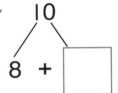
10
8 + ☐

5.
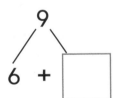
9
6 + ☐

6.
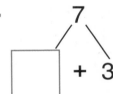
7
☐ + 3

7.
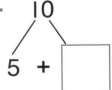
10
5 + ☐

8.
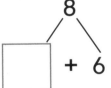
8
☐ + 6

9.
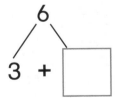
6
3 + ☐

10.
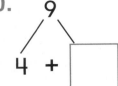
9
4 + ☐

11.
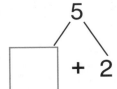
5
☐ + 2

12.
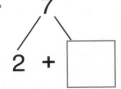
7
2 + ☐

Name _____

Going Further

1. Make three different **Math Mountains** with a total of 10.

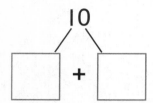 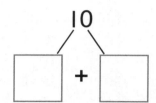 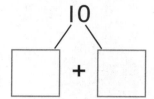

2. Make three different Math Mountains with a total of 8.

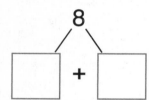 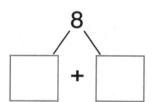 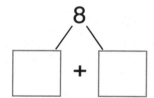

3. Make three different Math Mountains with a total of 7.

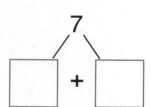 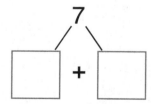 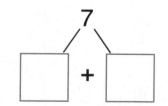

CA Standards: NS 1.3 Explore Unknowns

Dear Family:

Your child has started a new unit on story problems. Because most children this age are not strong readers, your child will probably need help reading the story problems. Offer help when it is needed, but do not give the answer.

To solve story problems, children first need to know which number is unknown. Is it the total or one of the parts? This program helps children focus on this important issue by introducing "Math Mountains." In a Math Mountain, the total sits at the top and the parts (or partners) sit at the bottom of the mountain. Children can quickly see the relationship between the partners and the total when they look at the mountain.

Math Mountain

Math Mountains are especially helpful in showing students how to find an unknown partner, as in the following problem: *I see 9 horses. 5 are black, and the others are white. How many horses are white?*

Children can find the answer by drawing the mountain to see which number is unknown. Then they count on from the partner they know to the total. In this way, they can find the partner they don't know.

Math Mountain with
Unknown Partner

4 more to 9

If you have any questions, please contact me.

Sincerely,
Your child's teacher

Estimada familia:

Su niño ha empezado una nueva unidad sobre problemas. Como la mayoría de los niños a esta edad no saben leer muy bien, es probable que su niño necesite ayuda para leer los problemas. Ofrezca ayuda cuando haga falta, pero no dé la respuesta.

Para resolver problemas, los niños primero deben hallar el número desconocido. ¿Es el total o una de las partes? Este programa ayuda a los niños a que se concentren en este punto importante presentándoles "Math Mountains" (Montañas matemáticas). En una montaña matemática el total está en la cima y las partes están al pie de la montaña. Al ver la montaña los niños pueden ver rápidamente la relación entre las partes y el total.

Montaña matemática

Las montañas matemáticas son especialmente útiles para mostrarles a los estudiantes cómo hallar una parte desconocida, como demuestra el problema siguiente: *Veo 9 caballos. 5 son negros y los demás son blancos. ¿Cuántos caballos son blancos?*

Los niños pueden hallar la respuesta dibujando la montaña para saber cuál es el número desconocido. Luego, cuentan hacia adelante a partir de la parte que conocen para hallar el total. De esta manera, pueden hallar la parte desconocida.

Montaña matemática
con parte
desconocida

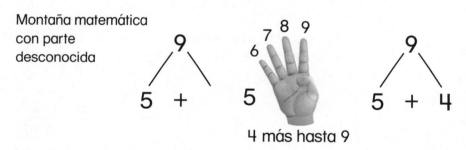

4 más hasta 9

Si tiene alguna pregunta, por favor comuníquese conmigo.

Atentamente,
El maestro de su niño

Explore Unknowns

Name _____

Class Activity

Vocabulary

story problems
label

Solve the **story problems**.	Show your work. Use pictures, numbers, or words.
1. We see 9 fish. 5 are big. The others are small. How many fish are small? [ ] _____ label	 fish
2. 8 boys are riding bikes. 6 ride fast. The rest ride slow. How many boys ride slow? [ ] _____ label	bike
3. Ana had 2 hats. Then she got more. Now she has 5. How many hats did she get? [ ] _____ label	 hat

4. Explain why it is important to write a **label** in the answer.

Going Further

1. Draw lines in this shape. Make 4 **triangles**.

2. Draw lines in this shape. Make 4 triangles.

3. Draw lines in this shape. Make 2 triangles.

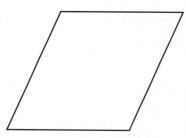

4. Draw lines in this shape. Make 2 triangles.

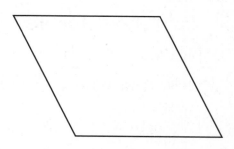

5. Explain How do you know the shapes you made are triangles?

CA Standards: MG 2.1   Stories with Unknown Partners

Name _____

Class Activity

Vocabulary

unknown partner
equation

Count on to find the **unknown partner**.

1. 3 + ☐ = 6

2. 7 + ☐ = 10

3. 2 + ☐ = 6

4. 7 + ☐ = 9

5. 4 + ☐ = 8

6. 5 + ☐ = 8

Count on to solve each exercise.

7. 6 letters total

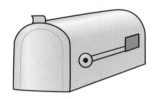

How many letters
are in the box?

☐ _____
label

8. 10 footprints total

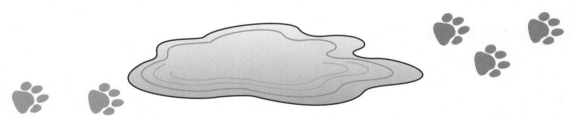

How many footprints
are under water?

☐ _____
label

➡ 9. **On the Back** Write an **equation** for
Exercise 8.

Solve Equations with Unknown Partners

$3 + \boxed{} = 6$	$3 + \boxed{} = 7$	$3 + \boxed{} = 8$
$3 + \boxed{} = 9$	$3 + \boxed{} = 10$	$4 + \boxed{} = 7$
$4 + \boxed{} = 8$	$4 + \boxed{} = 9$	$4 + \boxed{} = 10$
$5 + \boxed{} = 8$	$5 + \boxed{} = 9$	$5 + \boxed{} = 10$
$6 + \boxed{} = 9$	$6 + \boxed{} = 10$	$7 + \boxed{} = 10$

$3 + \boxed{5} = 8$

$\boxed{3 | \bullet\bullet\bullet\bullet\bullet}$

$3 + \boxed{4} = 7$

$\boxed{3 | \bullet\bullet\bullet\bullet}$

$3 + \boxed{3} = 6$

$\boxed{3 | \bullet\bullet\bullet}$

$4 + \boxed{3} = 7$

$\boxed{4 | \bullet\bullet\bullet}$

$3 + \boxed{7} = 10$

$\boxed{3 | \bullet\bullet\bullet\bullet\bullet}$

$3 + \boxed{6} = 9$

$\boxed{3 | \bullet\bullet\bullet\bullet\bullet\bullet}$

$4 + \boxed{6} = 10$

$\boxed{4 | \bullet\bullet\bullet\bullet\bullet\bullet}$

$4 + \boxed{5} = 9$

$\boxed{4 | \bullet\bullet\bullet\bullet\bullet}$

$4 + \boxed{4} = 8$

$\boxed{4 | \bullet\bullet\bullet\bullet}$

$5 + \boxed{5} = 10$

$\boxed{5 | \bullet\bullet\bullet\bullet\bullet}$

$5 + \boxed{4} = 9$

$\boxed{5 | \bullet\bullet\bullet\bullet}$

$5 + \boxed{3} = 8$

$\boxed{5 | \bullet\bullet\bullet}$

$7 + \boxed{3} = 10$

$\boxed{7 | \bullet\bullet\bullet}$

$6 + \boxed{4} = 10$

$\boxed{6 | \bullet\bullet\bullet\bullet}$

$6 + \boxed{3} = 9$

$\boxed{6 | \bullet\bullet\bullet}$

Yellow Count-On Cards

Number Quilt 2: Unknown Partners

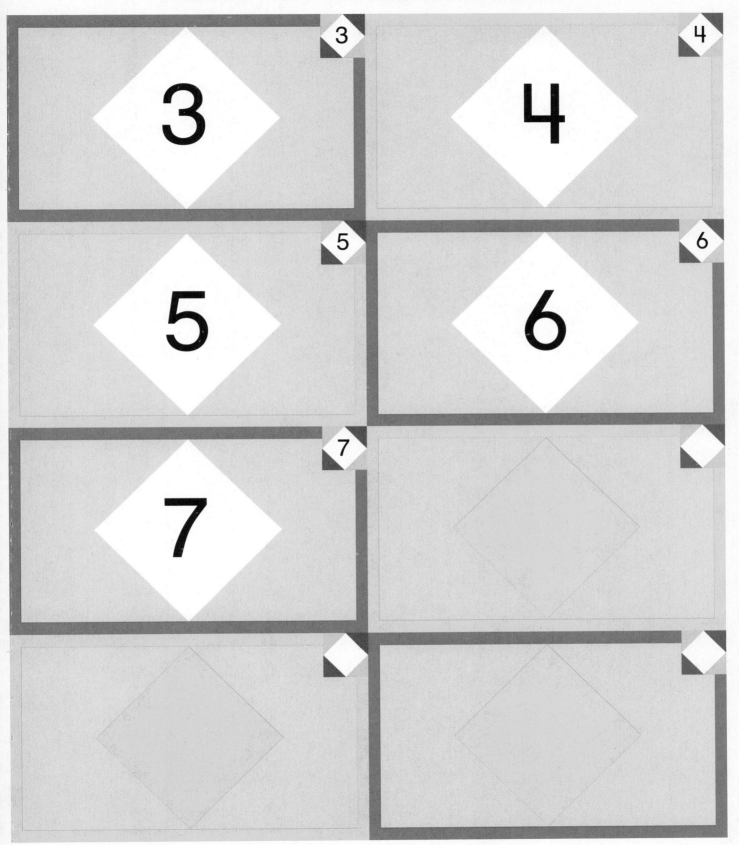

Use with the Yellow or Orange Count-On Cards.

Name _____

Going Further

Ring **more** or **less**. Tell why.

1. 3 + 4

   Will the answer be more or less than 10?   more   less

   Why? _____

2. 7 + 8

   Will the answer be more or less than 10?   more   less

   Why? _____

3. 2 + 3

   Will the answer be more or less than 10?   more   less

   Why? _____

4. 6 + 9

   Will the answer be more or less than 10?   more   less

   Why? _____

5. 4 + 4

   Will the answer be more or less than 10?   more   less

   Why? _____

6. **On the Back** Make up an addition equation with a total more than 10. Then make up another equation with a total less than 10.

Addition Game: Unknown Partners

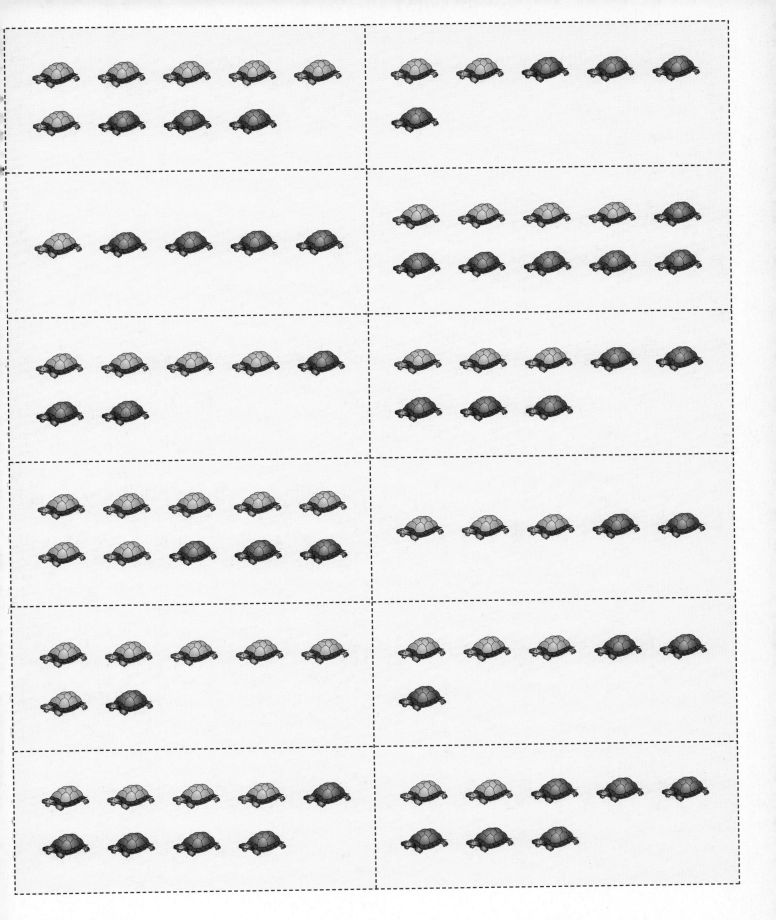

Practice with Unknown Partners

Name _____

Class Activity

subtraction story problems

Solve the **subtraction story problems**.

Show your work. Use pictures, numbers, or words.

1. 8 flies were on a log.
   6 were eaten by a frog.
   How many flies are left?

   ☐ _____
   　　label

   frog

2. I found 7 shells by the sea.
   Then I lost 3 of them.
   How many shells do I have now?

   ☐ _____
   　　label

   shell

3. I drew 10 houses.
   Then I erased 5 of them.
   How many houses are left?

   ☐ _____
   　　label

   house

➡ 4. **On the Back** Write a subtraction story.

Name

Subtraction Strategies

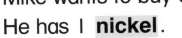
Going Further

Name _____

Vocabulary
nickel
pennies

Solve the story problems.

Show your work.

1. Mike wants to buy a toy car. 7¢
He has 1 **nickel**.
How many **pennies** does he need?

☐ _____
label

2. Mia wants to buy some toy rings.  2¢
She has 1 nickel and 1 penny.
How many rings can she buy?

☐ _____
label

3. Ben wants to buy some toy dogs.
He has 1 nickel and 3 pennies.  4¢
How many dogs can he buy?

☐ _____
label

 4. **On the Back** Write and solve your own coin story problem.

Subtraction Stories

$6 - 3 = \Box$

$7 - 3 = \Box$

$8 - 3 = \Box$

$9 - 3 = \Box$

$10 - 3 = \Box$

$7 - 4 = \Box$

$8 - 4 = \Box$

$9 - 4 = \Box$

$10 - 4 = \Box$

$8 - 5 = \Box$

$9 - 5 = \Box$

$10 - 5 = \Box$

$9 - 6 = \Box$

$10 - 6 = \Box$

$10 - 7 = \Box$

Orange Count-On Cards **99**

$8 - 3 = \boxed{5}$

$3 \;|\; \bullet\bullet\bullet\bullet\bullet$

$7 - 3 = \boxed{4}$

$3 \;|\; \bullet\bullet\bullet\bullet$

$6 - 3 = \boxed{3}$

$3 \;|\; \bullet\bullet\bullet$

$7 - 4 = \boxed{3}$

$4 \;|\; \bullet\bullet\bullet$

$10 - 3 = \boxed{7}$

$3 \;|\; \bullet\bullet\bullet\bullet\bullet\bullet\bullet$

$9 - 3 = \boxed{6}$

$3 \;|\; \bullet\bullet\bullet\bullet\bullet\bullet$

$10 - 4 = \boxed{6}$

$4 \;|\; \bullet\bullet\bullet\bullet\bullet\bullet$

$9 - 4 = \boxed{5}$

$4 \;|\; \bullet\bullet\bullet\bullet\bullet$

$8 - 4 = \boxed{4}$

$4 \;|\; \bullet\bullet\bullet\bullet$

$10 - 5 = \boxed{5}$

$5 \;|\; \bullet\bullet\bullet\bullet\bullet$

$9 - 5 = \boxed{4}$

$5 \;|\; \bullet\bullet\bullet\bullet$

$8 - 5 = \boxed{3}$

$5 \;|\; \bullet\bullet\bullet$

$10 - 7 = \boxed{3}$

$7 \;|\; \bullet\bullet\bullet$

$10 - 6 = \boxed{4}$

$6 \;|\; \bullet\bullet\bullet\bullet$

$9 - 6 = \boxed{3}$

$6 \;|\; \bullet\bullet\bullet$

100 UNIT 3 LESSON 8

Orange Count-On Cards

Going Further

Ring **more** or **less** . Tell why.

1. $10 - 4$

   Will the answer be more than or less than 10?   more   less

   Why? _____

2. $10 - 2$

   Will the answer be more than or less than 5?   more   less

   Why? _____

3. $10 - 7$

   Will the answer be more than or less than 5?   more   less

   Why? _____

4. $10 - 6$

   Will the answer be more than or less than 10?   more   less

   Why? _____

5. $10 - 3$

   Will the answer be more than or less than 5?   more   less

   Why? _____

6. **On the Back** Make up a subtraction equation with an answer more than 5. Then make up another one with an answer less than 5. Explain your thinking.

Subtraction Game: Unknown Partner

Going Further

1. Color the triangles one color. Color the squares a different color. Draw and color the next row in the **pattern**.

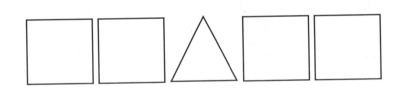

2. What would one more row of the pattern look like? Draw or write your answer.

➡ **3. On the Back** Use pattern blocks to draw and color a pattern.

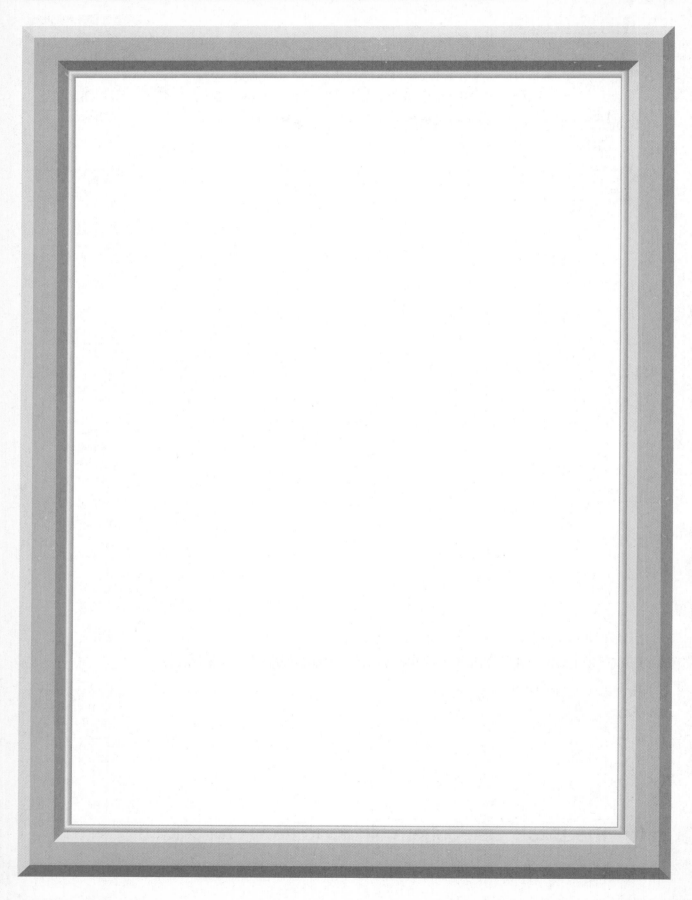

Practice with Subtraction Stories

Solve.

1. Sam scored 4 points. Julio scored 3 points. How many points did they score in all?

2. Sam scored 4 points. Julio also scored some points. In all they scored 7 points. How many points did Julio score?

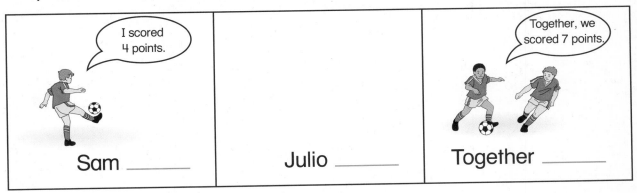

3. Sam scored some points. Then Julio scored 3 points. In all they scored 7 points. How many points did Sam score?

Going Further

Name _____

1. Mato had 5 toy cars.

   His friend gave him 3 more toy cars.

   How many toy cars does he have now?

   Write an equation to solve.

      = [ ]

2. Write your own story problem.

   _____

   -

   _____

   -

   _____

   -

   Write an equation for your problem.

      =

3. Did you make a plan to solve your problem? Explain.

   _____

   -

   _____

CA Standards: KEY NS 2.1; AF 1.1 Stories with Mixed Unknowns

Number Quilt 3: Any Unknown

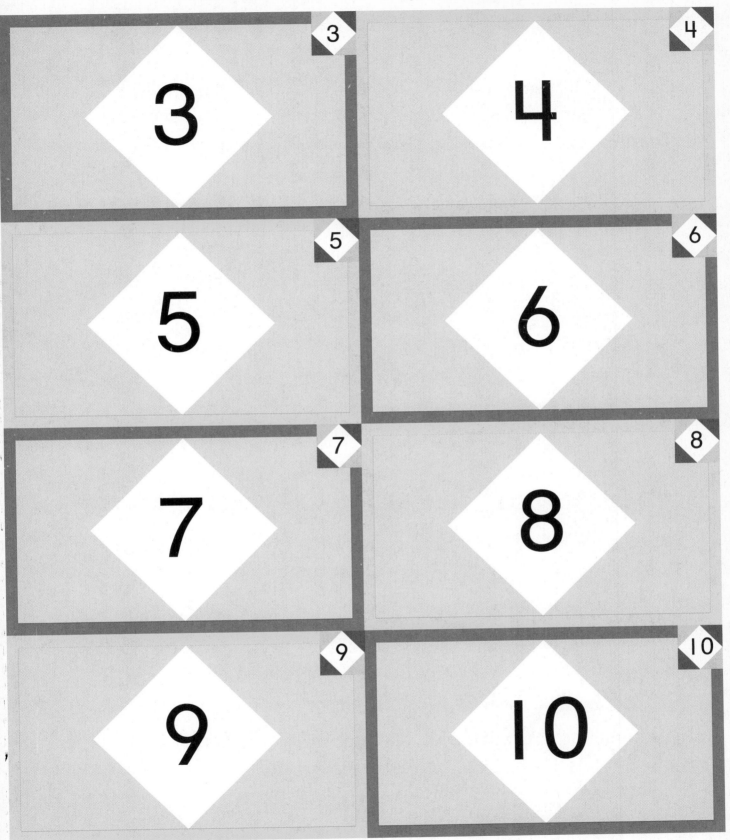

Use with any of the Count-On Cards.

Going Further

Solve each equation.

Cut out one addition equation and one subtraction equation.
Paste each equation onto a sheet of paper.
Draw a picture and solve.

7 + 1 = ☐	9 − 7 = ☐
1 + 8 = ☐	8 − 2 = ☐
3 + 2 = ☐	3 − 1 = ☐
6 + 3 = ☐	5 − 2 = ☐
4 + 5 = ☐	7 − 3 = ☐

Name _____

Find the unknown partner or total. Watch the signs.

1. $2 + 3 =$ ☐

2. $5 + 4 =$ ☐

3. $4 +$ ☐ $= 10$

4. $5 +$ ☐ $= 8$

5. $7 - 3 =$ ☐

6. $10 - 2 =$ ☐

7. $8 - 6 =$ ☐

8. $4 - 1 =$ ☐

Solve the story problems.

Show your work. Use pictures, numbers, or words.

9. Dinah had 2 seashells. Then she found 3 more. How many seashells does she have now?

seashell

☐ _____
label

10. There were 5 bees in the garden. Then 4 more bees came. How many bees are there in all?

garden

☐ _____
label

Name _____

Solve the story problems.

Show your work. Use pictures, numbers, or words.

---

11. Al put 3 pens on the table. He put the rest on the shelf. Altogether there are 9 pens. How many are on the shelf?

pen

☐ _____
label

---

12. There were 5 swans. Then 3 more swans came. How many swans are there now?

swan

☐ _____
label

---

13. Laura had 1 nickel. Then she found 3 pennies. How many cents does she have now?

nickel

☐ ¢

---

14. Molly had 1 nickel and 1 penny. She found 3 more pennies. How many cents does she have now?

penny

☐ ¢

Test

Name _____

Solve the story problems. | Show your work. Use pictures, numbers, or words.

---

15. Sam had 9 kittens. He gave 6 away. How many are left?

☐ _____
label

kitten

---

16. Rosa picked 6 carrots. Her sister picked some too. Together they picked 10 carrots. How many did Rosa's sister pick?

☐ _____
label

carrot

---

17. There were 5 rabbits in a field. Then 3 ran away. How many rabbits are left?

☐ _____
label

rabbit

---

18. Ed had 7 flowers in a vase. Then he gave 4 away. How many flowers are in the vase now?

☐ _____
label

vase

Solve the story problems.

Show your work. Use pictures, numbers, or words.

19. Ed had 1 nickel and 4 pennies. He spent 3 pennies on a button. How many cents does he have now?

button

☐ ¢

20. **Extended Response** Write a story problem about pennies. Solve your story problem using pictures, numbers, or words.

_____

- -

_____

- -

_____

- -

_____

- -

_____

4-1

Name _____

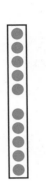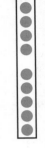

Vocabulary
tens

How many circles? Count by **tens**.

1.

_____ _____ _____ _____ _____ _____ _____ _____

Total

Add 1 ten.

 2.

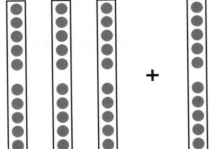 +

3.

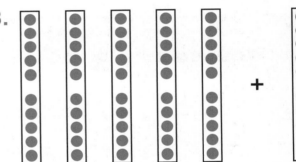 +

Equation _____

Equation _____

4. 70 + 10 = [ ]

5. 60 + 10 = [ ]

6. 20 + 10 = [ ]

7. 90 + 10 = [ ]

8. **On the Back** If you add 10 to an unknown number, the total is 90. Is the unknown number 70, 80, or 90? How do you know? Write or draw your answer.

Introduction to Tens Groupings

Dear Family:

Your child is learning about place value and numbers to 100. In this program, children begin by counting tens: 10, 20, 30, 40, and so on. They use a 10 × 10 Grid to help them "see" the relationship between the tens digit in a decade number and the number of tens it has.

10 20 30 40

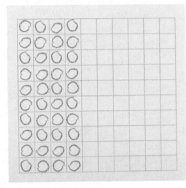

40 is 4 tens.

Soon, children will link 2-digit numbers to tens and extra ones. They will learn that a 2-digit number, such as 46, is made up of tens and ones, such as 40 and 6. Next, children will use what they know about adding 1-digit numbers to add 2-digit numbers.

$$3 + 4 = 7, \text{ so } 30 + 40 = 70.$$

Finally, they will learn to regroup and count on to find a total. For example:

$$19 + 5 = \boxed{24}$$

20
⟨19⟩ ○ ○ ○ ○ ○ 24

Right now, your child may enjoy counting by tens for you. He or she may also enjoy using household items to make groups of ten and extra ones, and then telling you the total number.

Sincerely,
Your child's teacher

Introduction to Tens Groupings **117**

Carta a la familia

Estimada familia:

Su niño está aprendiendo sobre valor posicional y los números hasta 100. En este programa, los niños empiezan contando decenas: 10, 20, 30, 40, etc. Usan una cuadrícula de 10 por 10 como ayuda para "ver" la relación entre el dígito de las decenas en el "número que termina en cero" y el número de decenas que tiene.

10 20 30 40

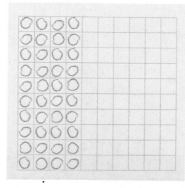

40 es 4 decenas.

En poco tiempo los niños harán la conexión entre números de 2 dígitos y decenas más otras unidades. A continuación aprenderán que un número de 2 dígitos, tal como 46, consta de decenas y unidades, como 40 y 6. Luego, los niños usarán lo que saben de la suma de números de 1 dígito para sumar números de 2 dígitos.

3 + 4 = 7, por lo tanto 30 + 40 = 70.

Finalmente, aprenderán a reagrupar y contar hacia adelante para hallar el total. Por ejemplo:

$$19 + 5 = \boxed{24}$$

20
(19) ○○○○○ 24

Por lo pronto, tal vez a su niño le guste contar en decenas para Ud. También puede divertirse al usar objetos del hogar para formar grupos de diez más otras unidades y luego decirle a Ud. el número total.

Atentamente,
El maestro de su niño

Introduction to Tens Groupings

Name _____

Going Further

Count by 2s.

1.

2   4   _____   8   10   _____   _____

Count by 3s.

2.

3   _____   _____   12   _____   18

Count by 4s.

3.

4   _____   _____   _____   _____   24

Represent Teen Numbers

Dear Family:

To help children "see" the tens and ones in 2-digit numbers, the *Math Expressions* program uses special drawings of 10-sticks to show tens, and circles to show ones. These images help children learn place value. Below are the numbers 27 and 52 shown with 10-sticks and circles:

Soon, you will see these 10-sticks and circles on the homework pages with instructions for children to write the number. Later, the 10-sticks and circles will be used to help children solve addition problems that require regrouping (sometimes called "carrying"). When there are enough circles to make a new ten, they are circled and then added like a 10-stick. The problem below shows 38 + 5:

Step 1: Show the two numbers with 10-sticks and circles

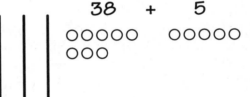

Step 2: Group the ones to make a new ten. Count by tens and ones.

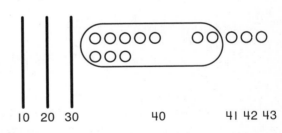

Right now, your child is just beginning to show teen numbers with 10-sticks and circles. He or she might enjoy drawing some for you. Soon your child will be able to draw 10-sticks and circles for any 2-digit number.

Sincerely,
Your child's teacher

Estimada familia:

Para ayudar a los niños a "ver" las decenas y las unidades en los números de 2 dígitos, el programa *Math Expressions* usa dibujos especiales de palitos de decenas para mostrar las decenas, y círculos para mostrar las unidades. Estas imágenes ayudan a los niños a aprender el valor posicional. Abajo se muestran los números 27 y 52 con palitos de decenas y círculos:

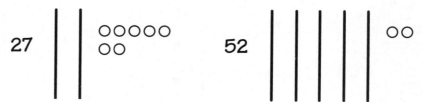

Los palitos de decenas y los círculos pronto aparecerán en las páginas de tarea donde se pedirá a los niños que escriban el número. Más adelante, los palitos de decenas y los círculos se usarán para ayudar a los niños a resolver problemas de suma que requieren reagrupar (que a veces se llama "llevar"). Cuando hay suficientes círculos para formar una nueva decena, se encierran éstos en un círculo y se suman como si fueran un palito de decena. El siguiente problema muestra 38 + 5:

Paso 1: Mostrar los dos números con palitos de decenas y círculos.

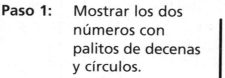

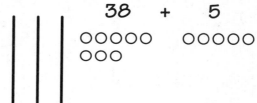

Paso 2: Agrupar las unidades para formar una nueva decena. Contar en decenas y unidades.

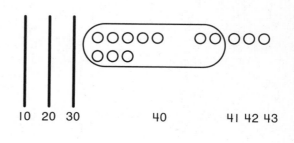

Por lo pronto su niño está apenas empezando a mostrar los números entre diez y veinte con palitos de decenas y círculos. Tal vez él quiera dibujar algunos para Ud. Pronto su niño podrá dibujar palitos de decenas y círculos para cualquier número de 2 dígitos.

Atentamente,
El maestro de su niño

Represent Teen Numbers

4-4

Extra Practice

Vocabulary
tens
ones

Find the total. Then make **tens** and extra **ones**.

1. 7 + 4 = ☐

  10 + ☐ = ☐

2. 8 + 8 = ☐

  10 + ☐ = ☐

3. 8 + 4 = ☐

  10 + ☐ = ☐

4. 9 + 6 = ☐

  10 + ☐ = ☐

5. 8 + 6 = ☐

  10 + ☐ = ☐

6. 5 + 7 = ☐

  10 + ☐ = ☐

7. 5 + 8 = ☐

  10 + ☐ = ☐

8. 2 + 9 = ☐

  10 + ☐ = ☐

9. **On the Back** Write two equations that show different partners for 13. Use 10 in one equation. Draw Stair Steps to show how you got your answers.

Visualize Teen Addition

$5 + 7 = \boxed{}$

$6 + 7 = \boxed{}$

$9 + 9 = \boxed{}$

$8 + 7 = \boxed{}$

$9 + 7 = \boxed{}$

$3 + 8 = \boxed{}$

$4 + 8 = \boxed{}$

$5 + 8 = \boxed{}$

$6 + 8 = \boxed{}$

$7 + 8 = \boxed{}$

$8 + 8 = \boxed{}$

$9 + 8 = \boxed{}$

$3 + 9 = \boxed{}$

$4 + 9 = \boxed{}$

$5 + 9 = \boxed{}$

$9 + 9 = \boxed{18}$

| 9 | •   ••••• |

$9 + 1 + 8$

$6 + 7 = \boxed{13}$

| 7 | •••   ••• |

$7 + 3 + 3$

$5 + 7 = \boxed{12}$

| 7 | •••   •• |

$7 + 3 + 2$

$3 + 8 = \boxed{11}$

| 8 | ••   • |

$8 + 2 + 1$

$9 + 7 = \boxed{16}$

| 9 | •   ••••• |

$9 + 1 + 6$

$8 + 7 = \boxed{15}$

| 8 | ••   ••••• |

$8 + 2 + 5$

$6 + 8 = \boxed{14}$

| 8 | ••   •••• |

$8 + 2 + 4$

$5 + 8 = \boxed{13}$

| 8 | ••   ••• |

$8 + 2 + 3$

$4 + 8 = \boxed{12}$

| 8 | ••   •• |

$8 + 2 + 2$

$9 + 8 = \boxed{17}$

| 9 | •   ••••• |

$9 + 1 + 7$

$8 + 8 = \boxed{16}$

| 8 | ••   ••••• |

$8 + 2 + 6$

$7 + 8 = \boxed{15}$

| 8 | ••   ••••• |

$8 + 2 + 5$

$5 + 9 = \boxed{14}$

| 9 | •   •••• |

$9 + 1 + 4$

$4 + 9 = \boxed{13}$

| 9 | •   ••• |

$9 + 1 + 3$

$3 + 9 = \boxed{12}$

| 9 | •   •• |

$9 + 1 + 2$

Green Make-a-Ten Cards

$6 + 9 = \boxed{}$

$7 + 9 = \boxed{}$

$7 + 4 = \boxed{}$

$8 + 4 = \boxed{}$

$9 + 4 = \boxed{}$

$6 + 5 = \boxed{}$

$7 + 5 = \boxed{}$

$8 + 5 = \boxed{}$

$9 + 5 = \boxed{}$

$5 + 6 = \boxed{}$

$8 + 9 = \boxed{}$

$7 + 6 = \boxed{}$

$8 + 6 = \boxed{}$

$9 + 6 = \boxed{}$

$4 + 7 = \boxed{}$

$7 + 4 = 11$

| 7 | ••• • |

$7 + 3 + 1$

$7 + 9 = 16$

| 9 | • ••••• |

$9 + 1 + 6$

$6 + 9 = 15$

| 9 | • ••••• |

$9 + 1 + 5$

$6 + 5 = 11$

| 6 | •••• • |

$6 + 4 + 1$

$9 + 4 = 13$

| 9 | • ••• |

$9 + 1 + 3$

$8 + 4 = 12$

| 8 | •• •• |

$8 + 2 + 2$

$9 + 5 = 14$

| 9 | • •••• |

$9 + 1 + 4$

$8 + 5 = 13$

| 8 | •• ••• |

$8 + 2 + 3$

$7 + 5 = 12$

| 7 | ••• •• |

$7 + 3 + 2$

$7 + 6 = 13$

| 7 | ••• ••• |

$7 + 3 + 3$

$8 + 9 = 17$

| 9 | • ••••••• |

$9 + 1 + 7$

$5 + 6 = 11$

| 6 | •••• • |

$6 + 4 + 1$

$4 + 7 = 11$

| 7 | ••• • |

$7 + 3 + 1$

$9 + 6 = 15$

| 9 | • ••••• |

$9 + 1 + 5$

$8 + 6 = 14$

| 8 | •• •••• |

$8 + 2 + 4$

Green Make-a-Ten Cards

Extra Practice

Name _____

Vocabulary
teen total
equation
solve

Find the **teen total**.

1. 5 + 9 = ☐

2. 10 + 5 = ☐

3. 7 + 4 = ☐

4. 9 + 10 = ☐

5. 9 + 8 = ☐

6. 9 + 9 = ☐

7. 3 + 9 = ☐

8. 7 + 8 = ☐

9. 10 + 4 = ☐

10. 6 + 5 = ☐

11. 8 + 8 = ☐

12. 8 + 4 = ☐

13. 7 + 6 = ☐

14. 9 + 7 = ☐

➡ 15. **On the Back** Write an **equation** with a teen total. Draw or explain how making a ten could help you **solve** your equation.

Teen Addition Strategies

Name _____

Going Further

Use the clues to solve each riddle.

1. • I am between 32 and 45.
   • I have 3 **ones**.
   • I have more than 3 **tens**.
   What number am I?

   [ ]

30	31	32	33	34	35	36	37	38	39
40	41	42	43	44	45	46	47	48	49

2. • I have more than 3 tens.
   • I am an even number.
   • I have as many tens as I have ones.
   What number am I?

   [ ]

30	31	32	33	34	35	36	37	38	39
40	41	42	43	44	45	46	47	48	49

3. • I am between 75 and 87.
   • I have fewer than 3 ones.
   • I am an odd number.
   What number am I?

   [ ]

70	71	72	73	74	75	76	77	78	79
80	81	82	83	84	85	86	87	88	89

4. **On the Back** Choose a 2-digit number.
   Write your own riddle. Use three clues.

Name _____

Integrate Tens and Ones

4-8

Going Further

Name _____

Solve the story problems. | Show your work. Use pictures, numbers, or words.

---

1. Tim has 14 pennies. He gets 8 more. How many pennies does he have?

_____ + _____ = [   ]

penny

---

2. There are 18 ducks. Then 5 more swim over. How many ducks are there now?

_____ + _____ = [   ]

duck

---

3. I saw 13 turtles on the rocks. I saw 9 turtles in the ponds. How many turtles did I see altogether?

_____ + _____ = [   ]

pond

---

4. Dan has 15 balls. Sue has 6 balls. How many balls do they have together?

_____ + _____ = [   ]

ball

---

5. **On the Back** Choose a problem you solved. Draw or write how you solved it.

UNIT 4 LESSON 8   CA Standards: KEY NS2.1   Practice Grouping Ones into Tens **133**

Copyright © Houghton Mifflin Company. All rights reserved.

Name

Practice Grouping Ones into Tens

1	2	10	20
1	2	1 0	2 0

3	4	30	40
3	4	3 0	4 0

5	6	50	60
5	6	5 0	6 0

7	8	70	80
7	8	7 0	8 0

9	90	100
9	9 0	1 0 0

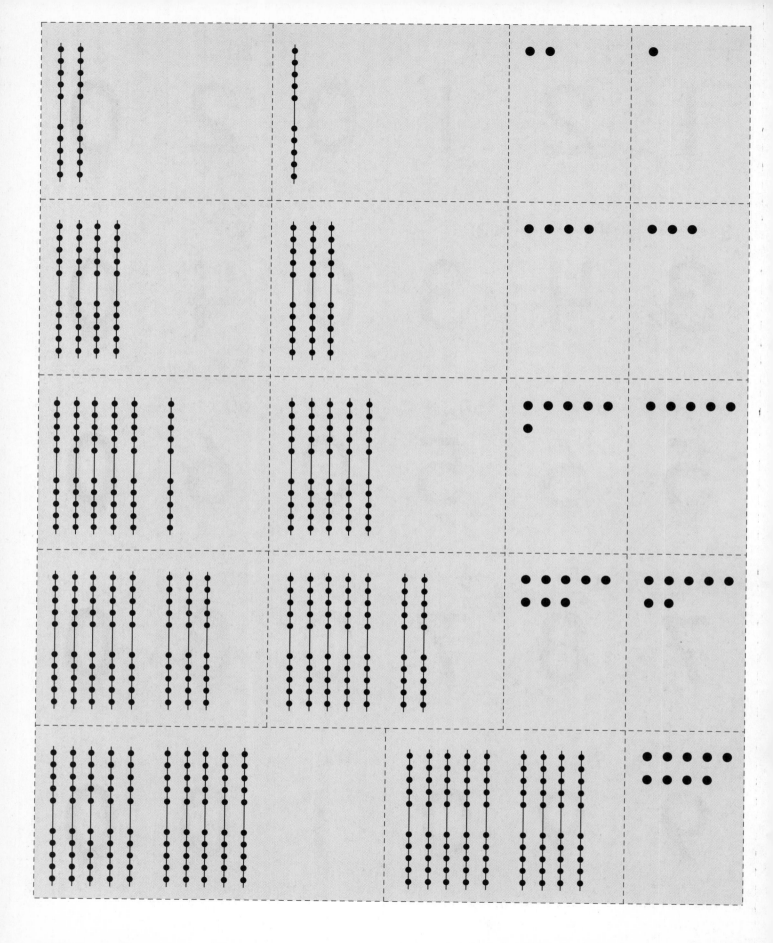

Secret Code Cards

Extra Practice

Vocabulary
equation

In the blank, write the number shown by the 10-sticks and circles. Then add the numbers.

1.

_____ + 10 = ▢

2.

_____ + 1 = ▢

3.

_____ + 10 = ▢

4.

_____ + 1 = ▢

5.

_____ + 1 = ▢

6.

_____ + 10 = ▢

 **7. On the Back** Choose a number greater than 10. Draw 10-sticks and circles to show it. Add 1 or 10 to the number. Write an **equation**.

Add Tens or Ones

Extra Practice

Name _____

Complete.

1. 3 + 6 = _____

   30 + 60 = _____

   30 + 6 = _____

2. 4 + 5 = _____

   40 + 50 = _____

   40 + 5 = _____

3. 2 + 4 = _____

   20 + 40 = _____

   20 + 4 = _____

4. 5 + 2 = _____

   50 + 20 = _____

   50 + 2 = _____

5. 7 + 2 = _____

   70 + 20 = _____

   70 + 2 = _____

6. 4 + 1 = _____

   40 + 10 = _____

   40 + 1 = _____

7. 3 + 2 = _____

   30 + 20 = _____

   30 + 2 = _____

8. 1 + 8 = _____

   10 + 80 = _____

   10 + 8 = _____

9. **On the Back** Write a set of 3 **equations**
   that follow the same rules as each set above.
   Then **solve** each equation.

CA Standards: NS 1.4, **KEY** NS 2.1

Mixed Addition with Tens and Ones

Extra Practice

Here is a riddle.

> I like to hop,
> but my ears are small.
> I have four legs, but I stand tall.
> I have a pocket,
> but I can't buy.
> Guess my name. Who am I?

Find the total. Use any method.

1. 46 + 5 = [   ] O

2. 40 + 2 = [   ] O

3. 19 + 5 = [   ] K

4. 24 + 4 = [   ] R

5. 64 + 6 = [   ] A

6. 20 + 9 = [   ] A

7. 27 + 5 = [   ] G

8. 89 + 2 = [   ] N

Who am I? Write the letter for each total.

_____ _____ _____ _____ _____ _____ _____ _____
 24   70   91   32   29   28   42   51

➡ **9. On the Back** Write or draw how
you solved Exercise 8.

Name _____

Counting On Strategy: 2-Digit Numbers

Write the number.

1. |||| ○ ○ [   ]

2. |||||| ○ ○ ○ ○ ○ ○ [   ]

Draw 10-sticks and circles.

3. 26

4. 71

---

5. How many flowers?

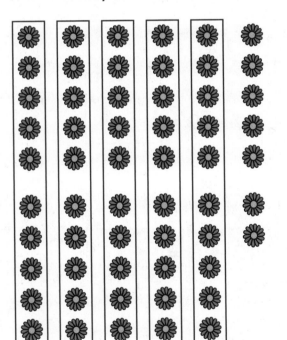

[   ]

6. How many pencils?

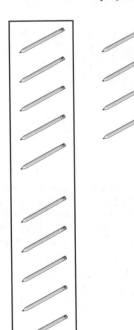

[   ]

Name _____

How many muffins?

Find the total.

7.

[ ]

8.
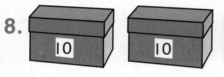 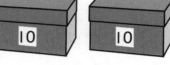

[ ]

9.

[ ]

10. 20 + 5 = [ ]

11. 52 + 6 = [ ]

12. 18 + 4 = [ ]

13. 37 + 9 = [ ]

14. 43 + 8 = [ ]

Test

 **4** **Unit Test**

Name _____

Solve the story problems.

Show your work. Use pictures, numbers, or words.

---

15. There are 10 bagels in a bag and 5 extra bagels. How many in all?

bagel

[ ] _____
label

---

16. Scott has a box of 10 pencils and 7 extra pencils. How many pencils does he have?

box

[ ] _____
label

---

17. There were 9 fish. Then 5 more fish came. How many fish are there now?

fish

[ ] _____
label

Name _____

18. There were 8 polar bears on the ice. Then 3 more came. How many polar bears are there now?

polar bear

☐ _____

Complete the exercises.

19. 40 + 2 = ☐

20. 4 + 2 = ☐

21. 40 + 20 = ☐

22. 30 + 6 = ☐

23. 3 + 6 = ☐

24. 30 + 60 = ☐

25. **Extended Response** Write a number greater than 10. Then draw 10-sticks and circles to show it.

Cut on dotted lines. **Fold** on solid lines and tape at top and bottom.

Dime Strips

Class Activity

Vocabulary
cents
coins

Ring 46 **cents**.

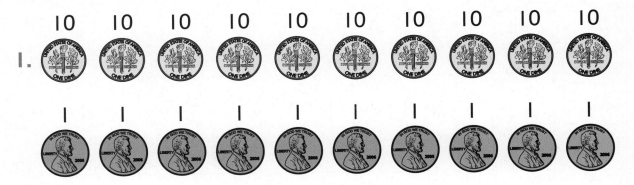

1.

Ring 83 cents.

2.

How many cents?

3.   [ ] ¢

4.   [ ] ¢

⟶ **On the Back** Suppose you have 24 cents.
You have no nickels. What **coins** could you
have? Write or draw your answers.

Explore Dimes and Pennies

Dear Family:

This unit builds upon what the class learned in Unit 4. Children continue to practice with 10-groups as they begin performing simple addition with tens and ones. Early in the unit, children apply this knowledge to the real world by learning about money. To add 8¢ and 5¢, for example, children will regroup the numbers as shown below.

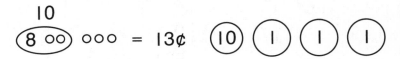

Later in the unit, children learn to add ten to any 2-digit number (38 + 10, for example). Then they learn to add multiple tens (38 + 40, for example). Using the Hundred Grid, shown below, allows children to see 10-based patterns in sequence.

1	11	21	31	41	51	61	71	81	91
2	12	22	32	42	52	62	72	82	92
3	13	23	33	43	53	63	73	83	93
4	14	24	34	44	54	64	74	84	94
5	15	25	35	45	55	65	75	85	95
6	16	26	36	46	56	66	76	86	96
7	17	27	37	47	57	67	77	87	97
8	18	28	38	48	58	68	78	88	98
9	19	29	39	49	59	69	79	89	99
10	20	30	40	50	60	70	80	90	100

3   ooo
13 | ooo
23 | | ooo
33 | | | ooo
43 | | | | ooo
53 | | | | | ooo
63 | | | | | | ooo
73 | | | | | | | ooo
83 | | | | | | | | ooo
93 | | | | | | | | | ooo

Children extend their work with tens and ones by using dimes and pennies to solve addition problems. Encourage your child to count coins at home.

If you have any questions or problems, please contact me.

Sincerely,
Your child's teacher

Estimada familia:

Esta unidad continúa lo que la clase estudió en la Unidad 4. Los niños siguen practicando con los grupos de 10 a medida que hacen sumas sencillas con decenas y unidades. Al comienzo de la unidad, los niños aplican estos conocimientos al mundo real cuando aprenden sobre el dinero. Para sumar 8 centavos y 5 centavos, por ejemplo, los niños reagrupan los números como se indica a continuación.

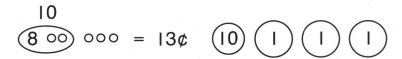

Más adelante en la unidad, los niños aprenden a sumar diez a cualquier número de 2 dígitos (38 + 10, por ejemplo). Luego aprenden a sumar varias veces diez (38 + 40, por ejemplo). Usando la cuadrícula de cien, que se muestra, los niños pueden ver en secuencia patrones de base 10.

1	11	21	31	41	51	61	71	81	91
2	12	22	32	42	52	62	72	82	92
3	13	23	33	43	53	63	73	83	93
4	14	24	34	44	54	64	74	84	94
5	15	25	35	45	55	65	75	85	95
6	16	26	36	46	56	66	76	86	96
7	17	27	37	47	57	67	77	87	97
8	18	28	38	48	58	68	78	88	98
9	19	29	39	49	59	69	79	89	99
10	20	30	40	50	60	70	80	90	100

3   ooo

13 | ooo

23 | | ooo

33 | | | ooo

43 | | | | ooo

53 | | | | | ooo

63 | | | | | | ooo

73 | | | | | | | ooo

83 | | | | | | | | ooo

93 | | | | | | | | | ooo

Los niños amplían su trabajo con decenas y unidades usando monedas de diez y de un centavo para resolver problemas de suma. Anime a su niño a contar monedas en casa.

Si tiene preguntas o dudas, por favor comuníquese conmigo.

Atentamente,
El maestro de su niño

Explore Dimes and Pennies

Going Further

Name _____

Vocabulary
pennies
coins
total

Draw the **pennies** you spin.

Ring the **coins** to make a ten if you can.

Count on to add. Write the **total**.

1.

Total

⬜ ¢

2.

Total

⬜ ¢

3.

Total

⬜ ¢

4.

Total

⬜ ¢

5.

Total

⬜ ¢

6.

Total

⬜ ¢

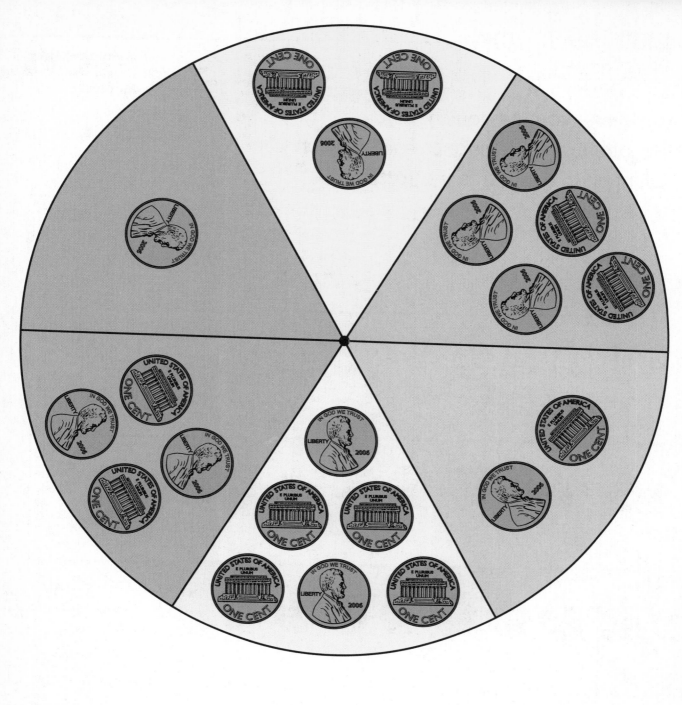

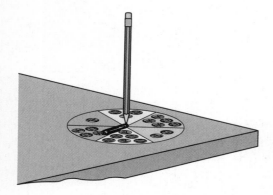

Group Pennies into Dimes

Class Activity

Name _____

1. Color each **10-group** a different color.
Count by tens and ones. Write the number.

➡️ **2. On the Back** Write a number between 11 and 100.
Then draw triangles to show that number.
Color each 10-group of triangles a different color.

Real-World Problems: Count with Groups of 10

Going Further

Name _____

Vocabulary

pattern
Hundred Grid

Think of the **patterns** from the **Hundred Grid**.
Write the missing numbers.

71	81	91	101	111
			102	112
			103	
	84			
75				
		96		
	87			
80		100		120

➡ **On the Back** Write the numbers from 31 through 80.
Write the numbers in columns of 10.

◖ **CA Standards: KEY** NS 1.1

Name _____

Create a Hundred Grid

Class Activity

Listen to the directions.

1	11	21	31	41	51	61	71	81	91
2	12	22	32	42	52	62	72	82	92
3	13	23	33	43	53	63	73	83	93
4	14	24	34	44	54	64	74	84	94
5	15	25	35	45	55	65	75	85	95
6	16	26	36	46	56	66	76	86	96
7	17	27	37	47	57	67	77	87	97
8	18	28	38	48	58	68	78	88	98
9	19	29	39	49	59	69	79	89	99
10	20	30	40	50	60	70	80	90	100

Going Further

Vocabulary
order
least
greatest

Write the numbers in **order** from **least** to **greatest**.

1. 20, 30, 10   _____ , _____ , _____

2. 30, 50, 40   _____ , _____ , _____

3. 20, 40, 30   _____ , _____ , _____

4. 70, 60, 50   _____ , _____ , _____

5. 60, 40, 50   _____ , _____ , _____

6. 80, 60, 70   _____ , _____ , _____

7. 50, 40, 30   _____ , _____ , _____

8. 30, 10, 20   _____ , _____ , _____

9. 90, 80, 70   _____ , _____ , _____

10. 80, 100, 90   _____ , _____ , _____

CA Standards: NS 1.0   Explore the Hundred Grid

Name _____

Class Activity

Vocabulary
Dime Strip   10-partner
Penny Array   100-partner

Listen.

Dime Strip

Penny Array

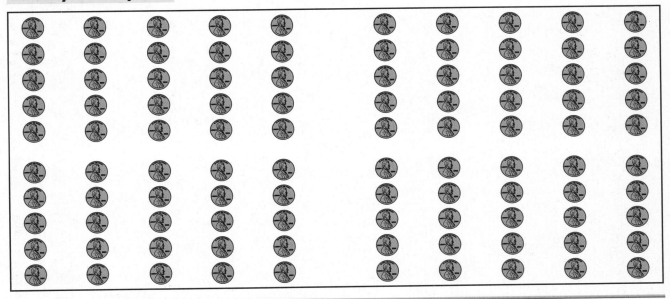

Find the **10-partners**.

1. _____ and _____

3. _____ and _____

5. _____ and _____

7. _____ and _____

9. _____ and _____

Find the **100-partners**.

2. _____ and _____

4. _____ and _____

6. _____ and _____

8. _____ and _____

10. _____ and _____

➡ **On the Back** Listen. Show how to solve the problem.

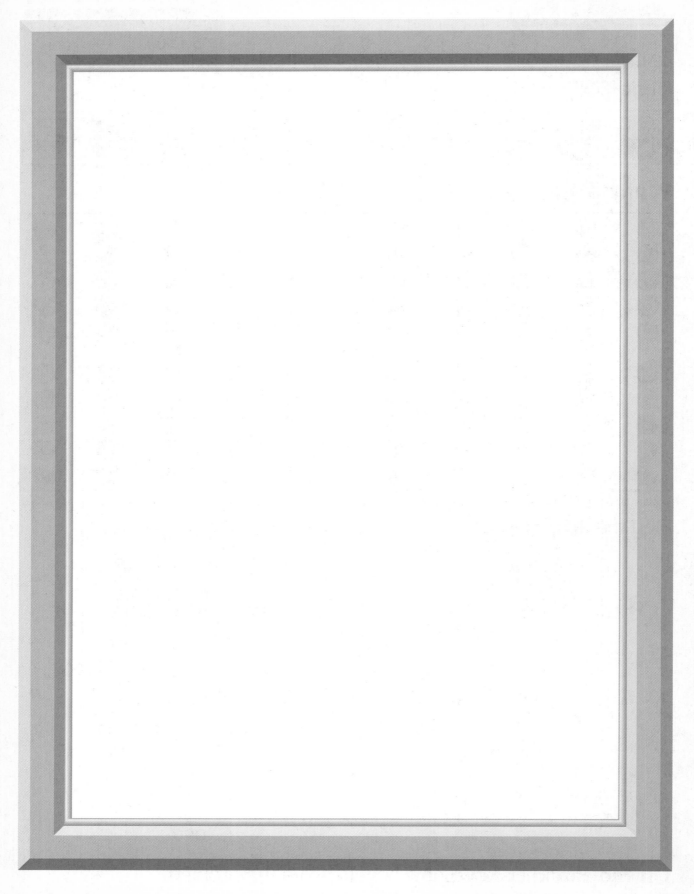

Partners of 100 and Dollar Break-Aparts

Class Activity

Use this page when you play the **Dime Detective** game.

10 dimes = 1 dollar

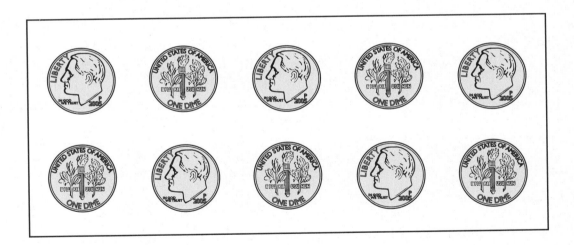

On the Back Draw 3 dimes. How many more dimes do you need to make 1 dollar? Explain how you know.

Solve Problems with Hundred Partners

Class Activity

Name _____

Vocabulary
amount
fewest

Ring pennies for each **amount**. Then draw dimes, nickels, and pennies for the amount. Use the **fewest** coins.

1. Peach
   38¢

2. Grapes
   46¢

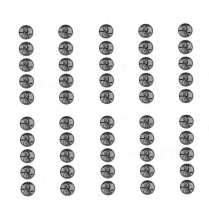

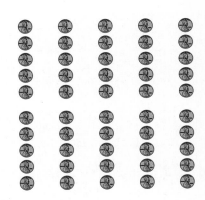

3. Melon
   52¢

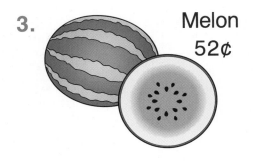

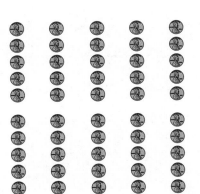

➡ **4. On the Back** Write a coin story problem.

Coin Combinations

$7 + \boxed{} = 16$ $6 + \boxed{} = 15$ $7 + \boxed{} = 11$

$8 + \boxed{} = 12$ $9 + \boxed{} = 13$ $6 + \boxed{} = 11$

$7 + \boxed{} = 12$ $8 + \boxed{} = 13$ $9 + \boxed{} = 14$

$5 + \boxed{} = 11$ $9 + \boxed{} = 18$ $7 + \boxed{} = 13$

$8 + \boxed{} = 14$ $9 + \boxed{} = 15$ $4 + \boxed{} = 11$

$7 + \boxed{4} = 11$

7 | ••• •
7 + 3 + 1

$6 + \boxed{9} = 15$

6 | •••• •••••
6 + 4 + 5

$7 + \boxed{9} = 16$

7 | ••• •••••
7 + 3 + 6

$6 + \boxed{5} = 11$

6 | •••• •
6 + 4 + 1

$9 + \boxed{4} = 13$

9 | • •••
9 + 1 + 3

$8 + \boxed{4} = 12$

8 | •• ••
8 + 2 + 2

$9 + \boxed{5} = 14$

9 | • ••••
9 + 1 + 4

$8 + \boxed{5} = 13$

8 | •• •••
8 + 2 + 3

$7 + \boxed{5} = 12$

7 | ••• ••
7 + 3 + 2

$7 + \boxed{6} = 13$

7 | ••• •••
7 + 3 + 3

$9 + \boxed{9} = 18$

9 | • ••••••••
9 + 1 + 8

$5 + \boxed{6} = 11$

5 | ••••• •
5 + 5 + 1

$4 + \boxed{7} = 11$

4 | •••••• •
4 + 6 + 1

$9 + \boxed{6} = 15$

9 | • •••••
9 + 1 + 5

$8 + \boxed{6} = 14$

8 | •• ••••
8 + 2 + 4

Purple Make-a-Ten Cards

$5 + \boxed{} = 12$ $6 + \boxed{} = 13$ $8 + \boxed{} = 17$

$8 + \boxed{} = 15$ $9 + \boxed{} = 16$ $3 + \boxed{} = 11$

$4 + \boxed{} = 12$ $5 + \boxed{} = 13$ $6 + \boxed{} = 14$

$7 + \boxed{} = 15$ $8 + \boxed{} = 16$ $9 + \boxed{} = 17$

$3 + \boxed{} = 12$ $4 + \boxed{} = 13$ $5 + \boxed{} = 14$

$8 + \boxed{9} = 17$

8 | •• :::
8 + 2 + 7

$6 + \boxed{7} = 13$

6 | •••• •••
6 + 4 + 3

$5 + \boxed{7} = 12$

5 | ••••• ••
5 + 5 + 2

$3 + \boxed{8} = 11$

3 | ••• •
3 + 7 + 1

$9 + \boxed{7} = 16$

9 | • :::
9 + 1 + 6

$8 + \boxed{7} = 15$

8 | •• •••••
8 + 2 + 5

$6 + \boxed{8} = 14$

6 | •••• ••••
6 + 4 + 4

$5 + \boxed{8} = 13$

5 | ••••• •••
5 + 5 + 3

$4 + \boxed{8} = 12$

4 | •••• ••
4 + 6 + 2

$9 + \boxed{8} = 17$

9 | • :::
9 + 1 + 7

$8 + \boxed{8} = 16$

8 | •• •••••
8 + 2 + 6

$7 + \boxed{8} = 15$

7 | ••• •••••
7 + 3 + 5

$5 + \boxed{9} = 14$

5 | ••••• ••••
5 + 5 + 4

$4 + \boxed{9} = 13$

4 | •••• •••
4 + 6 + 3

$3 + \boxed{9} = 12$

3 | ••• ••
3 + 7 + 2

Purple Make-a-Ten Cards

Name _____

Extra Practice

Match the **equation** to the picture that shows how to make a ten. Write the **unknown partner** in the box.

1. $8 + \boxed{} = 12$

9	• ••

2. $9 + \boxed{} = 15$

7	••• ••

3. $7 + \boxed{} = 12$

9	• •

4. $8 + \boxed{} = 14$

8	•• ••

5. $9 + \boxed{} = 12$

8	•• ••••

6. $8 + \boxed{} = 15$

9	• •••••

7. $9 + \boxed{} = 11$

9	• •••••••

8. $9 + \boxed{} = 17$

8	•• •••••

9. **On the Back** Explain how you matched each equation with its picture.

Unknown Addends with Teen Totals

$15 - 6 = \boxed{}$ $16 - 7 = \boxed{}$ $11 - 7 = \boxed{}$

$12 - 8 = \boxed{}$ $13 - 9 = \boxed{}$ $11 - 6 = \boxed{}$

$12 - 7 = \boxed{}$ $13 - 8 = \boxed{}$ $14 - 9 = \boxed{}$

$11 - 5 = \boxed{}$ $17 - 8 = \boxed{}$ $13 - 7 = \boxed{}$

$14 - 8 = \boxed{}$ $15 - 9 = \boxed{}$ $11 - 4 = \boxed{}$

$11 - 7 = \boxed{4}$

| 7 | ••• | • |

$7 + 3 + 1$

$16 - 7 = \boxed{9}$

| 7 | ••• | ••••• |

$7 + 3 + 6$

$15 - 6 = \boxed{9}$

| 6 | •••• | ••••• |

$6 + 4 + 5$

$11 - 6 = \boxed{5}$

| 6 | •••• | • |

$6 + 4 + 1$

$13 - 9 = \boxed{4}$

| 9 | • | ••• |

$9 + 1 + 3$

$12 - 8 = \boxed{4}$

| 8 | •• | •• |

$8 + 2 + 2$

$14 - 9 = \boxed{5}$

| 9 | • | •••• |

$9 + 1 + 4$

$13 - 8 = \boxed{5}$

| 8 | •• | ••• |

$8 + 2 + 3$

$12 - 7 = \boxed{5}$

| 7 | ••• | •• |

$7 + 3 + 2$

$13 - 7 = \boxed{6}$

| 7 | ••• | ••• |

$7 + 3 + 3$

$17 - 8 = \boxed{9}$

| 8 | •• | ••••••• |

$8 + 2 + 7$

$11 - 5 = \boxed{6}$

| 5 | ••••• | • |

$5 + 5 + 1$

$11 - 4 = \boxed{7}$

| 4 | •••• | • |

$4 + 6 + 1$

$15 - 9 = \boxed{6}$

| 9 | • | ••••• |

$9 + 1 + 5$

$14 - 8 = \boxed{6}$

| 8 | •• | •••• |

$8 + 2 + 4$

Blue Make-a-Ten Cards

12 − 5 = ☐ 13 − 6 = ☐ 18 − 9 = ☐

15 − 8 = ☐ 16 − 9 = ☐ 11 − 3 = ☐

12 − 4 = ☐ 13 − 5 = ☐ 14 − 6 = ☐

15 − 7 = ☐ 16 − 8 = ☐ 17 − 9 = ☐

12 − 3 = ☐ 13 − 4 = ☐ 14 − 5 = ☐

$18 - 9 = \boxed{9}$

9 | • ▓ | •••• / ••••
9 + 1 + 8

$13 - 6 = \boxed{7}$

6 | •••• / ••• ▓
6 + 4 + 3

$12 - 5 = \boxed{7}$

5 | ••••• / •• ▓
5 + 5 + 2

$11 - 3 = \boxed{8}$

3 | •••• / •••• | • ▓
3 + 7 + 1

$16 - 9 = \boxed{7}$

9 | • ▓ | ••••• /
9 + 1 + 6

$15 - 8 = \boxed{7}$

8 | •• ▓ | ••••• /
8 + 2 + 5

$14 - 6 = \boxed{8}$

6 | •••• / •••• ▓
6 + 4 + 4

$13 - 5 = \boxed{8}$

5 | ••••• / ••• ▓
5 + 5 + 3

$12 - 4 = \boxed{8}$

4 | ••••• / •• ▓
4 + 6 + 2

$17 - 9 = \boxed{8}$

9 | • ▓ | ••••• / •
9 + 1 + 7

$16 - 8 = \boxed{8}$

8 | •• ▓ | ••••• /
8 + 2 + 6

$15 - 7 = \boxed{8}$

7 | ••• ▓ | ••••• /
7 + 3 + 5

$14 - 5 = \boxed{9}$

5 | ••••• / •••• ▓
5 + 5 + 4

$13 - 4 = \boxed{9}$

4 | •••••• / ••• ▓
4 + 6 + 3

$12 - 3 = \boxed{9}$

3 | ••••• / •• ▓
3 + 7 + 2

Blue Make-a-Ten Cards

Match each **equation** with the picture that shows how to use the **Make a Ten strategy** .

1. 12 − 8 = ☐ | 7 | ••• ••• |

2. 14 − 9 = ☐ | 8 | •• •••• |

3. 13 − 7 = ☐ | 8 | •• •• |

4. 15 − 8 = ☐ | 7 | ••• •• |

5. 14 − 8 = ☐ | 9 | • •••• |

6. 12 − 7 = ☐ | 6 | •••• •••• |

7. 11 − 9 = ☐ | 8 | •• ••••• |

8. 14 − 6 = ☐ | 9 | • • |

9. **On the Back** Explain how you matched the equations with the pictures.

Subtraction with Teen Numbers

Going Further

Vocabulary

Math Mountain
equation

Complete the **Math Mountain**. Then write an
equation to match your Math Mountain.

1. 13

□ + □

Equation: _____

2. □

9 + □

Equation: _____

3. □

□ + 6

Equation: _____

4. 14

□ + □

Equation: _____

➡ **5. On the Back** Choose one exercise.
Explain how you completed the Math
Mountain and wrote the equation.

Mixed Practice with Teen Problems

Going Further

Name _____

Draw a line to the picture that shows how the
Make a Ten strategy can help you solve the **equation**.

1. $8 + \boxed{} = 14$

| 8 | ••   • |

2. $7 + 5 = \boxed{}$

| 6 | •••• ••••• |

3. $8 + 3 = \boxed{}$

| 8 | ••   •••• |

4. $6 + \boxed{} = 15$

| 7 | •••   ••• |

5. $9 + \boxed{} = 18$

| 9 | •   ••••• |

6. $9 + \boxed{} = 15$

| 8 | ••   •• |

7. $8 + 4 = \boxed{}$

| 9 | •   ••••••••• |

8. $7 + 6 = \boxed{}$

| 7 | •••   •• |

9. **On the Back** Write the equation $9 + 4 = \boxed{}$.
Then draw a picture that shows how to use the
Make a Ten strategy to solve it.

Name

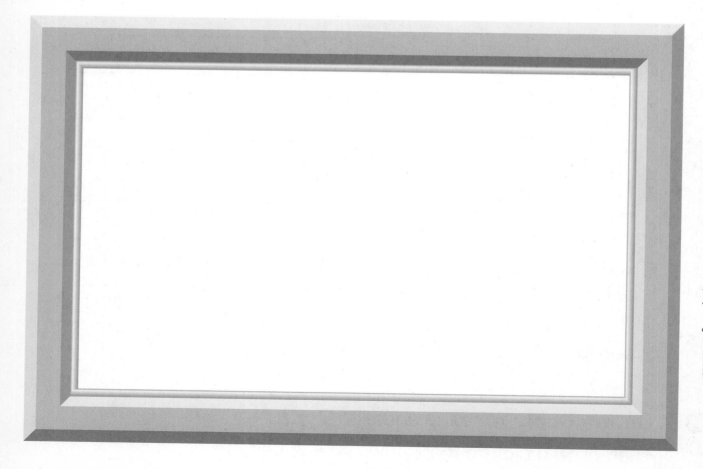

Small Group Practice: Teen Story Problems

Dear Family:

In Units 4 and 5, your child has been solving teen addition and subtraction problems by counting all or by counting on. Now your child is moving beyond these methods and working with a new method called the **Make-a-Ten strategy.** The strategy is explained below.

In a teen addition problem such as 9 + 5, children break apart the lesser number to make a ten with the greater number. Because 9 + 1 = 10, they break apart 5 into 1 + 4. Then they add the extra 4 onto 10 to find the total. A similar method is used to find unknown addends with teen totals and in teen subtraction. Children look for ways to make a ten because it is easier to add onto 10.

In the *Math Expressions* program, Make-A-Ten Cards help children use this method. Each card has a problem on the front. The back shows the answer and illustrates the Make-a-Ten strategy using pictures of dots. Below the pictures are corresponding numbers to help children understand how to make a ten. Practice the method with your child. As you continue to practice the Make-a-Ten strategy with your child, your child will become more adept at using mental math.

If you have any question about the Make-a-Ten strategy, please contact me.

Sincerely,
Your child's teacher

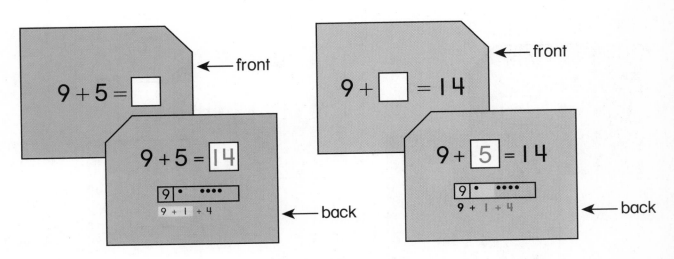

Make-a-Ten Cards

![Carta a la familia]

Estimada familia:

En las Unidades 4 y 5 su niño ha resuelto problemas de suma y de resta de números del 11 al 19 contándolos todos o contando hacia adelante. Ahora su niño está progresando más allá de estos métodos y está trabajando con un método nuevo que se llama la **Estrategia de hacer decenas**. La estrategia se explica a continuación.

En un problema de suma con números del 11 al 19, tal como 9 + 5, los niños separan el número más pequeño para formar una decena con el número más grande. Como 9 + 1 = 10, separan el 5 en 1 + 4. Luego suman al 10 los 4 que sobran para hallar el total. Un método semejante se usa para hallar sumandos desconocidos con totales entre el 11 y el 19 y con restas de números del 11 al 19. Los niños buscan maneras de formar una decena porque es más fácil sumar al 10.

En el programa *Math Expressions* las tarjetas para hacer decenas ayudan a los niños a usar este método. Cada tarjeta tiene un problema en una cara. En el reverso se muestra la respuesta y se ilustra la estrategia de hacer decenas mediante dibujos de puntos. Debajo de los dibujos hay números correspondientes para ayudar a los niños a que hagan una decena. Practique Ud. el método con su niño. A medida que practican juntos, su niño obtendrá más habilidad con el cálculo mental.

Si tiene alguna pregunta sobre la estrategia de hacer decenas, por favor comuníquese conmigo.

Atentamente,
El maestro de su niño

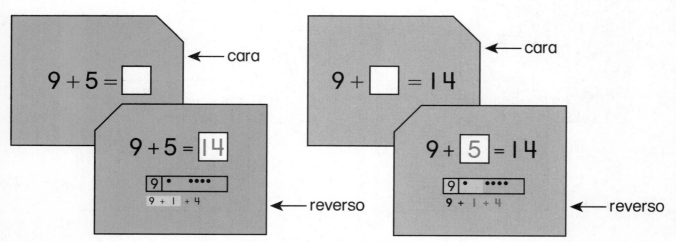

Tarjetas de hacer decenas

Small Group Practice: Teen Story Problems

Name _____

How many cents?

    10   10   10   1   1   1

1.     ¢

2.   ¢

3.   ¢

Continue the pattern.

4. | 12 | 22 | 32 | | | | | |

5. (27) (37) (47) ◯ ◯ ◯ ◯ ◯

6. 19 29 39 ...

7. 14 24 34 ...

Name _____

Solve the story problems.

Show your work. Use pictures, numbers, or words.

8. There were 15 ducks on the pond. Then 9 flew away. How many ducks are there now?

pond

☐ _____
label

9. Ed picked 7 apples and Joe picked 8. How many apples in all?

apple

☐ _____
label

10. Jan has 12 toy cars. 6 of them are red. How many of them are not red?

toy car

☐ _____
label

11. Peg planted 8 trees this morning and 6 trees this afternoon. How many trees did she plant today?

tree

☐ _____
label

Test

Name _____

Add the numbers.

12. 54 + 20 = ☐

13. 17 + 60 = ☐

14. 68 + 30 = ☐

15. 29 + 10 = ☐

Find the unknown 100-partner.

16. 40 + ☐ = 100

17. 70 + ☐ = 100

18. 90 + ☐ = 100

19. 20 + ☐ = 100

Complete the exercises. Watch the signs.

20. 8 + 5 = ☐

21. 13 − 4 = ☐

22. 14 − 6 = ☐

23. 9 + ☐ = 16

24. Draw the fewest coins for the amount.

Lettuce 57¢

25. Extended Response Suppose you have 33 cents. You have no nickels. What coins could you have? Write or draw your answer.

Glossary

5-group

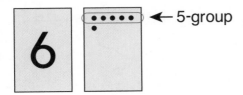

10-group

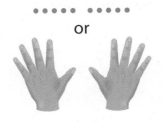

or

10-stick

There are 3 **10-sticks** in 32.

A

above

The sun is **above** the cloud.

add

$$3 + 2 = 5$$

addend

$$5 + 4 = 9$$

addends

addition story problem

There were 5 ducks.
Then 3 more came.
How many ducks are there now?

after

98, 99

99 is **after** 98.

apart

Amy pulls her hands **apart**.

Glossary (Continued)

B

backward

Sahil is walking **backward**.

before

31, 32

31 is **before** 32.

behind

Sara   Alex

Alex is **behind** Sara.

below

The sun is **below** the cloud.

between

Sam   Nadia   Lilly

Nadia is **between** Sam and Lilly.

7, 8, 9

8 is **between** 7 and 9.

break-apart

You can **break apart** the number 4.

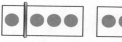

1 and 3   2 and 2   3 and 1

1 and 3, 2 and 2, and 3 and 1 are the **break-aparts** of 4.

C

cent

1¢

A penny is worth 1 **cent**.

centimeter

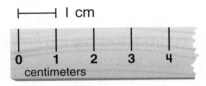

A **centimeter** cube is 1 centimeter long.

circle

circle graph

How I Spent 1 Dollar

coin

Quarters, dimes, nickels, and pennies are **coins**.

column

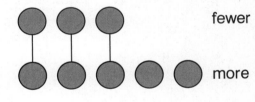

1	11	21	31	41	51	61	71	81	91
2	12	22	32	42	52	62	72	82	92
3	13	23	33	43	53	63	73	83	93
4	14	24	34	44	54	64	74	84	94
5	15	25	35	45	55	65	75	85	95
6	16	26	36	46	56	66	76	86	96
7	17	27	37	47	57	67	77	87	97
8	18	28	38	48	58	68	78	88	98
9	19	29	39	49	59	69	79	89	99
10	20	30	40	50	60	70	80	90	100

compare

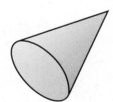

fewer

more

There are more red counters.
There are fewer blue counters.

cone

Glossary (Continued)

corner

corner

cost

What is the **cost** of the teddy bear?

The teddy bear **costs** 4¢.

count

1   2   3

count all

$$5 + 4 = \boxed{9}$$

• • • • •   • • • •

1 2 3 4 5   6 7 8 9

counting all

count on

$$5 + 4 = \boxed{9}$$

$$5 + \boxed{4} = 9$$

$$9 - 5 = \boxed{4}$$

5 • • • •
     6 7 8 9

Count on from 5 to get the answer.

cube

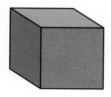

cylinder

D

decade numbers

10, 20, 30, 40, 50, 60, 70, 80, 90

difference

$$11 - 3 = 8$$

$$\begin{array}{r} 11 \\ -3 \\ \hline 8 \end{array}$$

difference →

dime

10¢ or 10 cents

dollar

1 **dollar** or 100 cents

Dot Array

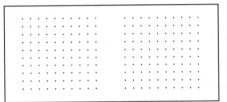

doubles

4 + 4 = 8

Both addends (or partners) are the same.

down

Put your arm **down**.

equal partners

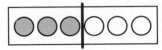

equal shares

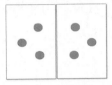

equal shares of 6

equal to (=)

4 + 4 = 8

4 plus 4 is **equal to** 8.

equation

Examples:

4 + 3 = 7   7 = 4 + 3

9 − 5 = 4   4 = 9 − 5

estimate

I **estimate** the paper clip is about 1 inch long.

Glossary (Continued)

even number

A number is even if you can make groups of 2 and have none left over.

8 is an **even number**.

F

fewer

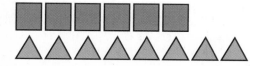

There are **fewer** ⬛ than △.

fewest

Eggs Laid This Month

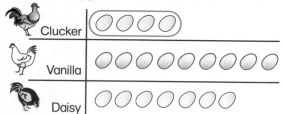

Clucker laid the **fewest** eggs.

forward

Sahil is walking **forward**.

fraction

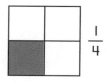

$\frac{1}{4}$

The **fraction** of the square that is shaded is $\frac{1}{4}$.

G

greater than

1, 2, 3, 4, 5, 6, 7

7 is **greater than** 3.

grid

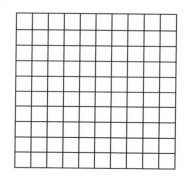

This is the Hundred **Grid**.

H

half-hour

A **half-hour** is 30 minutes.

hour

An **hour** is 60 minutes.

hundred

I	II	21	31	41	51	61	71	81	91
2	12	22	32	42	52	62	72	82	92
3	13	23	33	43	53	63	73	83	93
4	14	24	34	44	54	64	74	84	94
5	15	25	35	45	55	65	75	85	95
6	16	26	36	46	56	66	76	86	96
7	17	27	37	47	57	67	77	87	97
8	18	28	38	48	58	68	78	88	98
9	19	29	39	49	59	69	79	89	99
10	20	30	40	50	60	70	80	90	100

or

I

in, inside

Evan's hand is **inside** the box.

inch

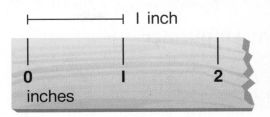

in front of

Alex   Sara

Sara is **in front of** Alex.

J

just after

5, 6, 7

6 is **just after** 5.

just before

4, 5, 6

5 is **just before** 6.

Glossary (Continued)

K

known partner

$5 + \boxed{} = 7$

5 is the **known partner**.

L

label

We see 9 fish.
5 are big. The others are small.
How many fish are small?

4 _____ fish
label

left

Cecilia is waving her **left** hand.

length

length

width

or

width

length

less

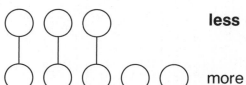

less

more

longer

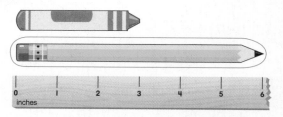

The pencil is **longer** than the crayon.

M

Make a Ten

$$8 + 6 = \boxed{}$$

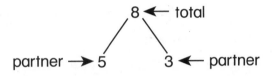

$10 + 4 = 14$,

So $8 + 6 = 14$.

Math Mountain

measure

Use the ruler to **measure** the paper clip.

minus

$$8 - 3 = 5 \qquad \begin{array}{r} 8 \\ -3 \\ \hline 5 \end{array}$$

8 **minus** 3 equals 5.

more

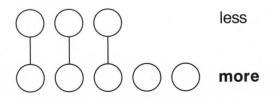

less

more

most

Eggs Laid This Month

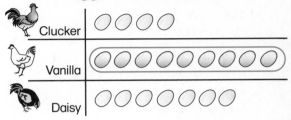

Vanilla laid the **most** eggs.

N

next to

Sara   Alex

Sara is **next to** Alex.

nickel

5¢ or 5 cents

not equal to (≠)

$6 \neq 8$

6 is **not equal to** 8.

Glossary (Continued)

number sentence

4 + 3 = 7
or
7 = 4 + 3

9 − 5 = 4
or
4 = 9 − 5

odd number

A number is odd if you can make groups of 2 and have one left over.

9 is an **odd number**.

one fourth

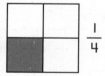

$\frac{1}{4}$

one half

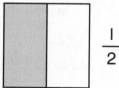

$\frac{1}{2}$

one third

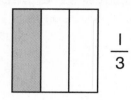

$\frac{1}{3}$

ones

ones

56 has 6 **ones**.

ordinal numbers

first, second, third, fourth, fifth
sixth, seventh, eighth, ninth, tenth

Ordinal numbers tell the position of things in order.

out, outside

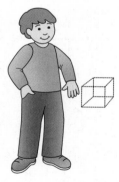

Evan's hand is **outside** the box.

oval

P

pair

a **pair** of counters

a **pair** of shoes

partner

5 = 2 + 3

2 and 3 are **partners** of 5.
2 and 3 are 5-**partners**.

Partner House

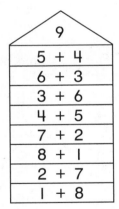

9
5 + 4
6 + 3
3 + 6
4 + 5
7 + 2
8 + 1
2 + 7
1 + 8

partner train

4-train

pattern

2, 4, 6, 8, 10, 12

These are **patterns**.

penny

1 ¢ or 1 cent

pentagons

A **pentagon** has 5 sides.

picture graph

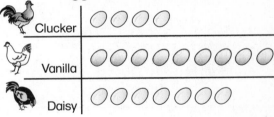

Eggs Laid This Month

Clucker	⬭⬭⬭⬭
Vanilla	⬭⬭⬭⬭⬭⬭⬭⬭
Daisy	⬭⬭⬭⬭⬭⬭

plus

3 + 2 = 5

$$\begin{array}{r} 3 \\ + 2 \\ \hline 5 \end{array}$$

3 **plus** 2 equals 5.

Glossary (Continued)

Q

quarter

25¢ or 25 cents

R

rectangles

rectangular prism

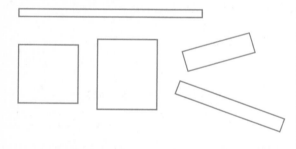

related equations

5 + 3 = 8
50 + 30 = 80

repeating pattern

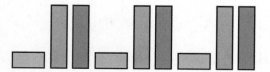

right

Cecilia is waving her **right** hand.

row

1	11	21	31	41	51	61	71	81	91
2	12	22	32	42	52	62	72	82	92
3	13	23	33	43	53	63	73	83	93
4	14	24	34	44	54	64	74	84	94
5	15	25	35	45	55	65	75	85	95
6	16	26	36	46	56	66	76	86	96
7	17	27	37	47	57	67	77	87	97
8	18	28	38	48	58	68	78	88	98
9	19	29	39	49	59	69	79	89	99
10	20	30	40	50	60	70	80	90	100

S

shapes

shorter

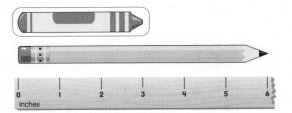

The crayon is **shorter** than the pencil.

side

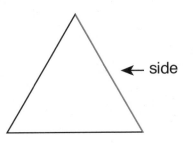

← side

sphere

squares

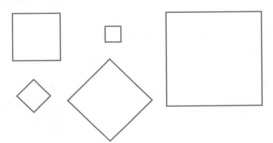

sticks and circles

1   ○

11 | ○

21 || ○

31 ||| ○

subtract

8 − 3 = 5

subtraction story problem

8 flies were on a log.
6 were eaten by a frog.
How many flies are left?

sum

4 + 3 = 7   4
                +3
total → →   7

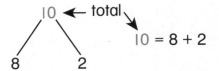

10 ← total
10 = 8 + 2

8   2

Glossary (Continued)

switch the partners

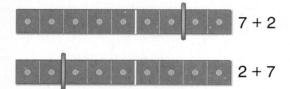

7 + 2

2 + 7

T

table

Instruments	Number
Horns	4
Violins	5
Drums	3
Guitars	5

teen number

11 12 13 14 15 16 17 18 19

teen numbers

teen total

$$14 \leftarrow \text{teen total}$$

9   5

tens

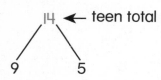

tens

56 has 5 **tens**.

together

Put your hands **together**.

total

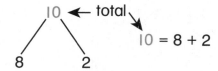

$$4 + 3 = 7$$

$$\begin{array}{r} 4 \\ + 3 \\ \hline 7 \end{array}$$

total →

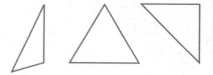

10 ← total

8   2

$$10 = 8 + 2$$

triangles

U

unknown partner

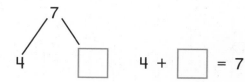

7

4   □

$$4 + □ = 7$$

unknown total

5   3   5 + 3 = ☐

up

Put your arm **up**.

vertical form

$$\begin{array}{r} 6 \\ +\ 3 \\ \hline 9 \end{array}$$

width

length

width

or

width

length

zero

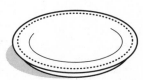

There are **zero** apples on the plate.